Guts and Go
Great Saskatchewan Hockey Stories

Guts and Go
Great Saskatchewan Hockey Stories

Calvin Daniels

Heritage
House

Copyright © 2004 Calvin Daniels

Library and Archives Canada Cataloguing in Publication
Daniels, Calvin, 1960-
Guts and go : great Saskatchewan hockey stories / Calvin Daniels.

ISBN 1-894384-80-6
1. Hockey--Saskatchewan. 2. Hockey players--Saskatchewan. I. Title.
GV848.5.A1D35 2004   796.962'097124   C2004-904755-8

Heritage House acknowledges the financial support for our publishing program from the Government of Canada through the Book Publishing Industry Development Program (BPIDP), Canada Council for the Arts, and the British Columbia Arts Council.

04 05 06 07/6 5 4 3 2 1

Heritage House Publishing
406-13th Avenue NE
Calgary, AB, Canada. T2E 1C2
ordering
Heritage House
#108-17665-66A Avenue
Surrey, BC, Canada. V3S 2A7
greatbooks@heritagehouse.ca
www.heritagehouse.ca

PRINTED IN CANADA

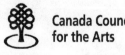

Contents

Foreword   9

Gritty Style Served Him Well   13
Saskatchewan's Own Golden Girls   19
Saskatchewan Tandem Anchors Islander Dynasty   27
The Smoke Eater from Saskatoon   35
A Step Taken into History   41
Red Baron Remembered for Double Hat Trick   48
It Was "Hammer" Time in Philly   54
Personal Tragedy Turns into Golden Moment   60
A Saskatchewan First   65
Bad Season, Good Memories   71
Hat Trick Welcomed to "The Show"   79
Longevity Marks Storied Career   85
Little Guy, Big Heart   90
Fulfilling Childhood Dreams   97
Even in Silence He Felt the Pride   103
Six-Decade Drought Ends   111
Cultural Component to Team   117
Net Results Were Usually Positive   124
An Eye for the Game   130
The Best of the West and All the Rest   135
The Tiger Had Claws   141

continued...

The Yin and Yang of the Yorkton Terriers   147
No Singing the Blues for Federko   153
Youth No Barrier to Centennial Cup Glory   159
Team Delivers Long-Coveted Cup to Town   166
Aboriginal Title Comes to Young Team   173
Cup Winner Cherished Memory   179
Brothers on Ice   184
Mr. Red Wing   193
Chevy Shines in Motor City   199
Sage of the SJHL   206
The Buckaroo From Bangor   213

Foreword

E ven though I have been a journalist for far too many years, writing a foreword for my second book is totally amazing and thrilling. When my first book, *Skating the Edge*, was released in 2001, I felt I had accomplished something, captured a little piece of immortality, inasmuch as a book will survive on a dusty shelf or two far longer than I'm likely to be around.

Then I got the call from Heritage House just days before Christmas in 2003, asking if I'd be interested in writing a book on Saskatchewan hockey. It was a natural follow-up to my collection of short stories on the sport in my first book, and was enticing in that the proposed book was to be a non-fiction work. As a journalist, I am familiar with the process of interviews and writing stories from those interviews, and the proposed book fit the mould nicely. So I said yes, although the time frame was only a few months long, which made me think about whether I *did* have time, given my day-to-day responsibilities as a newspaper and magazine writer. But the opportunity to seek out and interview the likes of Clark Gillies, Dave Schultz, and Tiger Williams was just too good to ignore.

So the process began. Immediately I knew the story of Saskatchewan hockey extended beyond those players who made it into the National Hockey League. While those players were easily recognizable to almost every hockey fan, there are hockey heroes in almost every town that has a rink in this province. Hockey transcends a sport here during the winter. It's a reason to get out of the house on frosty nights, a cure for cabin fever. The rink becomes a meeting place to discuss Christmas presents, where the ice fishing is good, and when spring might actually return. The game is more than goals and skating, too. It becomes a matter of community pride, bragging rights, and coffee shop fodder for the morning after.

In this book I hope I've been able to tell the stories of some of the heroes of the games played in hundreds of rinks in Saskatchewan since the days before artificial ice. I'm sure you'll recognize some, and understand why others are included here as you read their stories. It was a process of discovery for me, in a sense, since talking with one player would often lead me to another person who deserved to be in the book.

The culture of hockey is certainly a deep and rich one in the province. Yes, there are many names not here—yet. All books have space limitations, and choices had to be made. The good news is, if enough of you read this volume, Volume II of *Guts and Go* may well be on the horizon. A list posted on my desk has some 35 names of players and teams I'd like one day to interview. In the meantime, I hope everyone enjoys reading this book as much as I did writing it.

GREAT SASKATCHEWAN HOCKEY STORIES

Guts and Go

Gritty Style Served Him Well

You might expect being the first overall selection in the 1985 amateur draft of the National Hockey League would add some pressure to a budding career. Living in Canada, you might also expect that going to the Toronto Maple Leafs in the draft as the top pick would add yet more pressure. Well, in 1985, Wendel Clark, a native of Kelvington, Saskatchewan, found himself in just that situation, but he indicated there was no more pressure on him than on any other player trying to make the NHL.

"I didn't care where I was going when I was drafted. I just wanted a place to play," said Clark, adding, "I think there's always pressure on any player, but the biggest pressure is what you put on yourself." Certainly, Clark knew he was going to be drafted after two great seasons patrolling the blue line for the Western Hockey League Saskatoon Blades. From 1983 to 85 Clark recorded 55 goals, 100 assists, and 155 points. "It was a lot of fun. It was a great group of guys," said Clark of his time in Saskatoon. "Granted, the Blades weren't a powerful team, but from Saskatoon owner Nate

Broadsky to general manager Daryl Lubiniecki, it was a great organization to play with."

It helped, too, that Clark's older brother Don had been a
Blade, and younger brother Kerry would eventually follow his
older siblings to wear the Saskatoon jersey. In 1985, Clark's play as
a Blade took him to the international stage. He was invited to the
camp of the Canadian Junior National team, which would travel
to Finland and win the World Junior Championships. "It was very
exciting," he said, adding that just making the team was a big step.
"It was another huge training camp. There were 60 guys trying to
see who was going to play."

Playing for his country was special for Clark, but it didn't hit
him when he put on the jersey for the first time. Instead, it came
to him as the anthem played. "Anytime you get to put the sweater
on, it's special. But when you're standing on the blueline, and they
are playing the national anthem, you really get the feeling you are
playing for your country."

With a gold medal in his possession, and a solid junior record, Clark knew he'd be drafted. "But I didn't know where. It
could have been anywhere in the top five or six. Even on draft day
it was still between two or three teams." When Clark's name was
called by the Leafs first overall, it was just a relief to be taking a
step up to the NHL, not a case of being picked by a Canadian
institution. While many kids adored a certain team—many the
Leafs—Clark said that was not his style. "I wasn't really a fan of
anybody in particular," he said. "I played it more than I watched
it. Hockey Night in Canada used to be on at six o'clock Saturday.
At six o'clock Saturday we were all out at the rink playing." So
being drafted was the important thing, not who did the picking.
Toronto, at least, was a favourite of his father's, but he, too, was
just happy his son had a place to try and crack the NHL.

Clark said that, naturally, attending his first NHL training camp in the fall of 1985 was exciting. Thankfully, it was buffered by a few familiar faces, such as Dan Hodgson, whom he had played against in the WHL, and Russ Courtnall, whom he had played with as a AAA Midget at Notre Dame College in Wilcox, Saskatchewan. "I played in Wilcox for two years with Notre Dame," said Clark. "We had a pretty good team."

Clark remembered the camp just to make the Midget Hounds. "There were about 140 kids from Saskatchewan and across Canada trying out for the team," he said, adding that it was different from back home in Kelvington, where everyone made a team just to ice a full roster. The Hounds, with Clark on defence, would compete in the Air Canada Cup, the Canadian AAA Midget Championship held in British Columbia, coming up just a little short of a win. "It was neat," he said of the national stage. "I always take everything in stride, though. I always just played hard no matter where I was. You always play as hard as you can, whether you're playing on a good team or a bad team."

As for arriving in Toronto, even his first trip to Maple Leaf Gardens was low-key for Clark, going in the back door for a player meeting. The hallowed halls of the Gardens didn't leave him in awe. "I didn't really know anything more about Maple Leaf Gardens and the Leafs at the time than I did about the Pittsburgh Penguins," he said.

Joining the Leafs did put Clark in an organization dominated at the time by owner Harold Ballard, who was often at odds with his players, the media, and the fans. "I got along very well with Harold. I think most players got along with Harold," he said, adding that when he was dealing with the often cantankerous former owner of the Leafs, he was only starting in the league. "I was 18, and just happy to be in the league." Clark said that had he been a long-time veteran, relations with the owner might have been more contentious. "But, in the big picture, I was treated very well by Harold Ballard and his family." At the same time, having Ballard as a very hands-on owner sometimes attracted a brighter spotlight to a team already the centre of attention because of its history and location.

Clark said that, as a player, he tried to avoid letting the swirls of controversy affect on him on the ice. "Players can only control what they do on the ice. You can't control what's outside the game," he said. On the ice, the Leafs at the time were a young squad, and Clark fit right in, although his years of being a blue-line patroller were over, as he was moved to forward almost immediately in Toronto. "It wasn't that bad. I was always a very offensive-minded defenceman anyways."

Helping ease the transition to forward was the fact he was put on a line with old Hound teammate Russ Courtnall and with Gary Leeman, who had also played in Wilcox prior to Clark's time there. The line—quickly tagged "The Hound Line"—melded together nicely. "We just had a lot of great energy," said Clark, adding that each player brought something to the unit. "Gary Leeman is one of the most talented players I've ever played with in any sport … Russ Courtnall was a speedster with a lot of flash." Clark's contribution was his trademark feisty grit. It was a style that both provided the rugged forward with an edge and took its toll on his overall career. "That's just the way I've always played. It just felt natural to go out and play hard, and play physical." Clark said his style meant playing through a lot of bumps, bruises, and more serious injuries. "Because of the way I played, starting way back in junior, not just the NHL, I missed a lot of games."

As it was, Clark had a solid rookie season, scoring 34 goals and adding 227 penalty minutes, showing both sides of his game style. It would be the start of a 15-year career, although he only played 793 regular-season games, missing more than 400 with injuries. The same injuries probably took a season or three off the end of his career as well. But Clark has no regrets. "The way I played was the way I had to play to play well."

The first 10 years of Clark's career were played in Toronto, and it looked like he might be a career Leaf. Then trade rumours swirled with his name attached for a couple of seasons. When they finally quieted, he was moved to the Quebec Nordiques on draft day in 1994. It was a move to a team on the rise, with young stars such as Owen Nolan and Joe Sakic. The Nordiques were on the move, as was seen in 1995–96 when the team relocated to Denver and became the Colorado Avalanche.

While some unilingual, English-speaking players regarded Quebec City as a difficult place to play because of the predominant French language, Clark said the transition was easy. "Hockey was the language, much like it is across Canada." Clark would move from the Nordiques after one season to go to New York and the Islanders before being back with the Leafs for another stint, traded again, and finally finishing in Toronto for the end of the 1999–2000 season. He finished with 330 goals, 234 assists, and 564 points, plus 1,690 penalty minutes. Clark said he might have hung on another season or two, but chose to walk away on his own terms. Still, it was a good run for a kid from Kelvington, a community that gave him lots of ice time to learn the key to hockey, how to skate. It's a part of the game he said can't be coached. "Before you are six, seven, eight, there's really not a lot you can coach kids. You never teach a kid to walk, they do it themselves. It's the same with skating. They need to learn balance and stuff on their own by just skating."

Once the skating was smooth for Clark, it was lots of hockey, too, playing on travelling and house-league teams in his hometown until bantam, when the miles on the family car started to add up. Clark began playing with a AA team in Yorkton, a 100-mile trip (160 km) one way for games and practices. It was a trip his parents never minded making, he said. "As long as I played, they were committed to helping." Clark looks back on his career with satisfaction, a satisfaction tinged with one huge regret—no Stanley Cup ring, although he made the semi-finals twice. "It was a disappointment, but that's hockey. There's a lot of great players who never got to drink from the Cup."

Saskatchewan's Own Golden Girls

It was a benchmark in women's hockey and a golden moment for Canada, and four Saskatchewan-born players were part of it. In 2002, Canada won the Olympic gold medal in women's hockey in Salt Lake City. Hayley Wickenheiser, Dana Antal, Kelly Béchard, and Colleen Sostorics stood on the blue line listening to the strains of their national anthem. The victory was huge for the sport in Canada and for the players on the ice.

Sostorics said she certainly didn't realize the importance it had taken back in her home country. "Call me naive, but I didn't really realize it would be as big a deal as it turned out," she said. "I knew my parents would be watching, but not seven million other Canadians." The players had to keep their emotions under some level of control. "At the time you're just playing hockey," said Sostorics. Béchard said the team simply didn't think Canada would be so moved by their win, in spite of knowing the game is popular. "I don't think any of us realized the impact it had on the people back in Canada. I don't think we realized that until we stepped off the plane."

Wickenheiser, one of the country's top players, always looked to the Olympics as the zenith of her sport. "For me it was always the premier event in women's hockey." Antal was actually cut prior to the 1998 Olympics, so "being told I was going to the Olympics (in '02) was obviously a dream come true." Béchard said the Olympics became a focussing point for her development as a hockey player. A member of Team Saskatchewan at the Canada Games, Béchard was scouted at age 17 to attend a national team training camp. Not only would she make the Canada under-22 team, but she would come to appreciate that hockey could lead her to the Olympics. She said having that goal helped her become a better player. "Hockey had always been a game that I loved, something I was very passionate about," she said. "I wanted to be the best player I could be ... Going to that camp really opened my eyes to what I needed to do to achieve that."

For many on the team, the 2002 gold medal was just a bit sweeter because it followed the bitterness of losing the gold medal game in Nagano, Japan, in 1998. "That was obviously bitter. It was tough, but it set us up well for 2002," said Wickenheiser. "We were hungry. We didn't want to experience that feeling from Nagano again. It was such a sick feeling standing on the blue line. In 2002, we had so many veterans who didn't want to feel the way they did in '98."

In 1998, Canada went into the gold-medal game as favourites, but were considered underdogs four years later, having lost eight meetings in a row with the American team leading up to their big game. "We had lost eight-of-eight to the Americans leading up to Salt Lake, but we all felt we could win that one game when it mattered the most," said Wickenheiser. Antal said she certainly felt the veterans' desire to win in Salt Lake. "All we had on our minds was winning a gold medal. There was a feeling they (the veterans) had made some mistakes in Nagano, and maybe some regrets ... I just kind of knew this time around, leaving the gold-medal game, win or lose, they would know they had played the best they could."

Still, the gold-medal game in 2002 was a nail-biter. The Canadians led 1–0 early on a goal by Caroline Ouellette, marking the first time the Americans had trailed in the tournament. Wickenheiser would make it 2–0 early in the second, before the Americans got their first. Then with time almost expired in the second, Jayna Hefford scored what would eventually be Canada's game winner, as they stayed up to win the game 3–2. "I never thought it was ours until there were zero seconds on the clock," said Wickenheiser, adding that the feeling of the win was "unbelievable."

It was clearly an emotional time for the team and the country they represented. "The pride was seeping out of my eyeballs," said Sostorics. "It was my happy place, too—the flag being raised, the national anthem being played, and the gold medal around your neck." The feeling almost escaped description for Béchard, who added that the emotion hit home as the final buzzer sounded. "It was the most pride you could ever feel hearing the national anthem played," she said. "You look down and your teammates are getting their gold medals, and then it's put around your neck—it's something I've dreamed about my whole athletic career. It's unbelievable."

Although they went into the game as underdogs, Béchard said there was a surprising relaxed calm around the team. "I think as a team we were all really prepared for the game. We knew as a team we had done everything we could to prepare for that game. We knew player-for-player we were definitely more talented. It was just a matter of putting everything together and playing an outstanding game." Antal said there "was no doubt" in her mind the team would be in the gold-medal game. She added that, while it might seem like arrogance, she expected to win. "I never thought we were going to lose that game after it started," she said. "There was a feeling when that puck dropped we were going to win that game." And when it was over there was almost relief, said Antal. "We were just unbelievably happy to have worked that hard and won. When you've worked so hard, it's so much more worthwhile in the end."

Going into the game, Sostorics said it was a case of trying to maintain the regime as it had been before any other game, playing hacky-sack and trying to stay loose. "I don't remember being particularly nervous. We were just going through the same routine," she said. Once the game started, penalties piled up for the Canadians, and Sostorics said it was a case of hitting the bench, "catching our breath and going back to kill another penalty." Killing the string of penalties actually allowed Sostorics a feeling the team "was doing all right" in the game. "It was kind of surreal how everybody presented themselves in different situations."

Each of the "golden girls" had similar starts in hockey. For Wickenheiser, it was almost in the genes. "Dad (Tom) played old-timer hockey and we used to go to the rink quite a bit," she said. "I can remember being pulled on my sled to the rink and asking my mom (Marilyn) if I could play hockey." The first step was a family backyard rink for Hayley and her siblings. From there it was a natural to start playing organized hockey in her hometown of Shaunavon. Of course, that meant playing with the boys. "I didn't see it as a big deal, having a girl playing hockey," she said, adding that, in a small town, "I was just another body to help make the team work."

For Antal, it was a case of her parents suggesting she might consider hockey. "My parents just asked me if I wanted to play hockey," she said, adding that it was somewhat unique. "Back then there weren't a lot of parents asking their daughters if they wanted to play hockey." In Esterhazy, Saskatchewan, that meant joining the boys on the ice, too. "I was really, really fortunate. The boys I played hockey with in Esterhazy were all kids I went to school with, so it didn't seem to matter whether I was a boy or a girl."

At four, Sostorics began to skate and play the game, but she doesn't have a personal recollection of why. "The story goes that I just asked if I could play. My parents put me in some of my older brother's old equipment and away I went." It was an immediate match, hockey and Sostorics. "I love everything about it. I love the ice, the fast pace, the physical play," she said. "It just feels right for me." Sostorics would play on the local boys' teams in Kennedy until she completed high school. The small town allowed her lots of ice time and playing with the boys forced her development because of their size and strength. "I could have been on the ice every day."

Béchard's older sister had started to play hockey on a team coached by an uncle, and Kelly quickly followed her lead. "I started playing when I was five. Growing up in a small town (Sedley, population 350) there's not a lot of kids to play," she said, adding that her sister was the draw. "Growing up, you always idolize your older siblings." The first all-female team for Béchard wasn't until she reached the age of 14, when she joined a bantam girls team in Regina, playing against peewee boys. "I remember it was very competitive."

As Wickenheiser grew older, she said there was the issue of dressing room space as she continued on boys' teams, and in some cases there were a few people jealous of the ice time a girl was taking away from the boys. "But my parents were great, they always sheltered me from that stuff. I think Mom and Dad heard some of that stuff, but they didn't worry me about it," she said.

As Antal got older, hockey lost its lustre for a time. In her first year of contact hockey, she found it wasn't something she enjoyed. "I really didn't enjoy it at all. I didn't really like being the only girl on a boys' team," she said. Antal would play a little girls' hockey, travelling literally hours for games, but she said her ice time was sporadic. "Once I started playing hockey with the girls, I didn't play a lot of organized games." Then, as Antal completed high school, Cornell University came calling. "At the time there weren't a lot of Canadian girls heading down to the U.S. colleges," she said, but she took the plunge, spending two seasons there. "It was not really a means to an end. It was just an opportunity which I decided to take."

Antal came back to Canada after being selected for the women's national program. "I was far from ready to be playing at the international level," she said. "I was released from that team after a couple of months." While admitting it was hard to accept she wasn't good enough, it set her on a mission. "I realized trying to make the national team was something I really had to go for." So she moved back to Calgary to play with the best players. "They were doing things quicker and faster and stronger. I was put in a position I had to do things at a higher level just to survive on a day-to-day basis." The work paid off when she made the 2002 team.

Sostorics also made a move after high school, heading to Calgary to play with the University of Calgary Dinosaurs and a senior women's team. Both were preludes to making the Canadian under-22 national team in 1998. She would play on the team for three years. She admitted the step up to the national stage was a big one. "I think every level you move up is a substantial jump. Everything is a little bit faster. You have to think a little bit faster," she said. Playing on the under-22 team was a great experience because it helped her prepare for the next step to the national team. "It gets the nerves of wearing the maple leaf on your sweater well over," she said. Pulling on the sweater for the first time certainly carries emotions with it. "It's something you've dreamed about and when you finally do it, it's an amazing feeling." In 2001, Sostorics made the national team, and it, too, was a big step. "We always say you're playing with the big girls now." Sostorics' selection was never totally expected, as she was one of 30 who started out. "You had to prove yourself that whole year. I was just working hard every day. I'm not sure it even crossed my mind that I'd be in the Olympics."

Béchard also headed to Calgary after high school with the goal of becoming a better hockey player and getting her education. She said the under-22 team was sort of a bridge to finally making the national team, where she won gold medals at the World Championships in both 2000 and 2001, events she said emotionally rivaled the Olympic victory for her.

Wickenheiser admitted that her skill level made her one of the better players on most teams she played on. Such skills also allowed her to dream a hockey dream she shared with almost every Canadian boy. "I always dreamed I would play in the NHL one day. I'd play with either the Oilers or the Canadiens," she said. However, by the time she was 11 or 12, Wickenheiser said she realized "it was going to be a lot more difficult being a female player in hockey." So her NHL dream faded. Then, in 1990, the first Women's World Hockey Championships were held. "I watched the 1990 World Championships in Calgary. I was very inspired by that," said Wickenheiser. A couple of years later, she was in British Columbia at a hockey school when more good news came. "Mom came running in and said women's hockey had been accepted as a gold-medal sport in the Olympics. I remember thinking from that point on, I had a purpose."

For Wickenheiser that purpose will continue as she plans to play in the 2006 Olympics and has an eye set on 2010 in Vancouver as well. Antal also wants to be back in 2006. "That's my goal right now, because it was such a positive experience in 2002," she said. Sostorics wants to go back, too, having nothing but good memories from Salt Lake City, both on the ice and off. She said just being part of the opening ceremonies was beyond words. "It was a sort of feeling that is very hard to explain." She remembers walking into the stadium and just to the left seeing a gathering of screaming, flag-waving Canadian supporters. "I don't know if I shed a tear, but I know I felt like it." Béchard wants the feeling of the Olympics at least once more. "I want to win another one and I want to be a more important part of that win. I think I still have a few years left to give to the team and to the program." Having four members of the gold-medal team from Saskatchewan doesn't surprise Wickenheiser. "I think Saskatchewan tends to produce hard-working, good character players."

Saskatchewan Tandem Anchors Islander Dynasty

For slightly more than half a decade, the New York Islanders were the toast of the National Hockey League, winning four Stanley Cups in a row and coming within a skate blade of making it five. The Isles were a team rich in talent, including two players whose careers culminated with inductions to the Hockey Hall of Fame—Bryan Trottier and Clark Gillies, both gritty forwards with a scoring touch from Saskatchewan.

For Trottier the call from the Hall of Fame was something nearly beyond belief. "You can dream about playing in the NHL. You can dream about scoring your first goal. You can dream about winning the Stanley Cup," he said. "But you never dared dream about making the Hall of Fame. That's beyond the possible." Walking up to accept the induction, Trottier said it was overwhelming in the sense that one recalls the excitement and sacrifice of a career. "It's impossible to put into words," he said.

The Hall of Fame call was an equally cherished moment by Gillies, although he was never sure it would come. "Friends were always saying, 'You're Hall of Fame material, you should be in there,'" he recalled. In his first year of eligibility, Gillies missed induction by only one vote. The second year it was a wider margin and his thoughts of induction sort of faded. Then it happened. "We were going back to Saskatchewan for my mom's 80th birthday," recalled Gillies. "I was in the airport checking calls back at the office." Among the messages was a number in Toronto. He made the call. It was Jim Gregory from the Hall of Fame who was looking for him, with the news of his selection. "I was sitting in the waiting room by myself when he told me. I was speechless. I basically started to cry right on the spot. I'm sure some people sitting around me thought I'd just got some really bad news." In fact, when his wife returned to join him, she, too, was worried the tears were because of bad news, but Gillies said he quickly assured her, "These are happy tears." He then called everybody he could think of with the news.

Gillies said entering the Hall was the perfect exclamation point to his career. "There's really nothing like getting into the Hall of Fame." He also found his induction to be a time of reflection. "You think a lot, going right back to the old rink at home, how we shovelled off the ponds, all the little tournaments in all the little towns, freezing your feet off at the outdoor rinks and crying your eyes out while they warmed up," he said.

Trottier was in Maine coaching when the call came. He, too, said it was unexpected, although friends and hockey people kept saying the call would come in 1997. Like Gillies, Trottier learned to skate on outdoor ice, in his case on the family ranch near Val Marie. "I think I was about six years old when we moved back there. There was a little creek that ran by the house. I learned to skate on that." Reflecting on his career, which spanned 1,279 regular-season games and 71 playoff games, Trottier said it all started on the creek back home, although as a boy he didn't realize where skating might lead him. "Going down to the creek back then, had somebody come along and said, 'You're going to play in the NHL one day,' I'd have said, 'Oh yeah?'" he said. "But I still went out there. We'd skate for an hour until our toes froze, then go home crying. As soon as we warmed up, it was back out. I couldn't understand why my sister didn't want to be out there all the time like I did."

Trottier said the Hall of Fame induction was another special moment, no more or less prized than a series of career milestones. He scored 524 regular-season goals, adding 901 assists for 1,425 points. Along the way he collected his share of NHL hardware, including the Calder Memorial Trophy as the league's top rookie in 1974–75, the Art Ross Trophy for top scorer in 1978–79 (with 134 points), and the Hart Memorial Trophy as NHL MVP the same season. Trottier said each award, each milestone, was something to be savoured, but also something he did not accomplish alone. "All those things are exciting, are rewarding individually," he said, "but you wouldn't get the awards and recognition if you didn't have talented guys around you, and a good organization behind you." Trottier pointed to the Calder Trophy and said if New York Islander coach Al Arbour had not given him ice time—he had 95 points as a rookie—the award would not have been possible.

For both players, the career in the NHL came after a good base in the game back home in Saskatchewan. Trottier said his organized hockey started when the Val Marie rink was built, although hockey started early. "I can still remember Dad buying me a Gordie Howe special stick at Art LaBell's, a little gift store in Val Marie," he said. The stick was for a right-handed shot, although nature would run its course and Trottier would be a left-handed player in time. "Dad said if I was going to follow in somebody's footsteps, then I should follow a player like Gordie." Once teams were established in Val Marie, the hockey was pretty good, and when they combined players with nearby Climax, the results were outstanding. "We'd (the two towns) join forces and go kick the crap out of all of Saskatchewan in provincial playoffs and a few tournaments," he said, adding that the team won several major titles when he played. By the time Trottier was a young teen, he was playing for three teams in the same season: his age-group team in Val Marie, the community's senior team (the Mustangs), as well as with the Swift Current Legionnaires. "That was probably the best year I had for development and for fun," he said, pointing first to the senior team. "There were only seven or eight guys on the team, so I got tons of ice time."

That's how it started for Gillies, too. While his career in the NHL may have spanned 958 games, in which he amassed Hall of Fame numbers of 319 goals, 378 assists, and 697 points, along with 1,023 penalty minutes, it started at five years of age in Moose Jaw. "As best I can recall I really started learning how to skate when I was five," he said. At the time his father challenged him to become a good skater first. He told his son that when he could come home and say he was able to skate without falling down, he would give him a new stick. Gillies looks back on that simple thing as an important step, suggesting that too often kids are rushed to start playing hockey before they fully grasp the fundamental of skating. "They start skating around leaning on their sticks and they don't really learn how to skate," he said, adding that kids need to skate lots when starting out. "I think that was good advice for me."

In Gillies' case, keeping him off the ice was the biggest challenge. "We had a corner rink I used to go to every single day, even in the dead of winter cold. At times we could actually skate up there on the ice on the street," he said. "It had to be a bitter cold day I didn't play hockey. I ate, drank, and lived hockey. It was just our life growing up." In the games on the streets and in outdoor makeup games, Gillies was a Chicago Blackhawk, as he liked their uniform and loved Bobby Hull most of all. "I always liked the look of number nine. It was all part of the reason I wore number nine myself." In time, Gillies began to watch the Montreal Canadiens. "I could really appreciate the way they played the game. I got a lot out of watching them."

While Gillies learned tricks on the outdoor rinks and by watching NHL teams on television, it was junior hockey with the Regina Pats that made him want to be a hockey player, especially the advice of Earl Ingarfield. "The guy really changed my attitude about hockey. He taught me a lot about how to play the game, but also about being an individual, about being a man, not a boy," he said. The advice included letting Gillies know he had the size, the toughness, the skills to go to the pros, if his mindset wanted it badly enough. "He said, 'You've got all the tools, you've just got to get it in your head you want to be a hockey player … It was at that time I realized I might have a future in the game."

Trottier, too, credited Ingarfield with helping him, coaching him in his third year of WCHL action in Lethbridge. "I was like a sponge whenever Earl was around. Whatever he said, I would try." While Trottier developed enough to draw attention as a junior, he admitted he might do things differently given another chance today. "You sacrifice a big portion of your young life to the game when you should be focussing on school," he said, "I'd probably finish up high school and go to college and try it that way." As it was, Trottier completed only a couple of Grade 11 credits and the rest of his education came through experience. He admitted that he missed school, which he liked. "I did a lot of reading in junior. I brought a dictionary along to figure out what some of the words meant," he said.

For Gillies, it didn't hurt to capture a Memorial Cup in his final season, 1973–74, as a Regina Pat. That same spring, he was drafted by the Islanders in the first round, number four overall. New York was in a building mode and he stepped right into the lineup as a 20-year-old rookie, never missing a game while scoring 25 goals and 47 points.

Trottier would first receive an offer from the Cincinnati Stingers of the World Hockey Association, who drafted him in 1974. The deal was for $50,000 a season for 10 years. "That was more money than my parents had ever seen, than any of us had ever seen," he said. However, a lawyer friend of the family suggested they wait to see if an NHL team was interested in Trottier, too, which suited the young forward's mindset. "I wasn't really gung-ho about playing in the WHA. I wanted to play in the NHL. I didn't care where." The Islanders selected Trottier in the second round, 22nd overall in the '74 draft. "My quick gut reaction was, here's an opportunity to be part of a young organization and maybe break in a bit quicker."

From the outset of their careers, Gillies and Trottier seemed tied together with the Islanders, lining up with sniper Mike Bossy to create one of the most dominant lines in the league for half a decade. "I played against Trotts when he was in Swift Current," said Gillies. "You could just see the talent this guy had. He was just a strong, hard-nosed, talented guy." Trottier likewise has admiration for Gillies. "Gilly has great hands for a big guy. I don't know if I've ever seen better hands," adding that his ability to work the puck to his linemates helped the line work as well as it did. With Bossy in the mix, the three clicked big-time. "It was a nice five-year stretch," said Gillies. "We each benefited from the others' play."

"Good things happen when you've got the guys that work their tails off," said Trottier. It was also a successful stretch for the Islanders, who jelled into the NHL's powerhouse franchise, winning their four Cups with a veteran lineup that stayed rather constant throughout the run. "It was disappointing to lose the fifth one against Edmonton, but the four we did win were a tribute to everybody that was there," said Gillies.

None of the Cups were any sweeter than the first, though, won in the spring of 1980. "The first one was so exciting. I can remember it like it was yesterday," said Gillies, adding that a defining moment came versus Boston, a team deep with rugged players. "That was the real turning point for us. We weren't going to be pushed around ... There was a lot of blood left on the ice after that series." It was just as tough against Philadelphia, beating the Flyers four games to two for the Cup. "To come out of those battles and be victorious was fulfilling," said Gillies. "We just never looked back." In 1981, the Isles defeated Minnesota 4–1 in the Stanley Cup finals, in 1982 it was 4–0 over Vancouver, and in '83 another sweep, this time over Edmonton.

Trottier said each Cup holds memories for him, each special for its own moments. He likened it to having kids—you don't love one more than the next, even if it was the first. "You love them all equally." Although both Gillies and Trottier will be forever remembered as Islanders, neither's career ended there. Gillies moved on to Buffalo and two rather disappointing seasons with the Sabres. Trottier was also let go. "They thought there was nothing left and I thought differently," said Trottier, who moved on to Pittsburgh, where he would twice more hoist the Stanley Cup at season's end—in both 1991 and 1992.

Finally, age and hundreds of hockey games left both Trottier and Gillies realizing that it was time to retire. In Trottier's case, his body was telling him, and it was a heartfelt desire for Gillies. After failing to win the fifth Stanley Cup, Gillies felt his edge wasn't there. Trottier's bad back meant more time in the trainer's room than on the ice. "I wasn't playing with reckless abandon anymore, and you need to in the NHL," he said.

For Gillies, retirement meant a complete career change, heading to the world of finance. Trottier didn't want to get that far from the game he said was mentally tough to leave. "The next best thing to it (playing) is coaching," he said. He has been an assistant with both Pittsburgh and Colorado in the NHL, and had a brief stint as the head coach with the New York Rangers.

Although both have had storied careers, they haven't forgotten their roots in Saskatchewan or their families. It was appropriate that Gillies learned of his Hall of Fame induction as he headed home to see his mother, although he admitted he failed in his attempt to keep it a secret from her until he arrived. Trottier also puts family first. "Nothing is better than being a dad—all the Stanley Cups, all the awards, the Hall of Fame—I'm a dad every day, and nothing beats that."

The Smoke Eater from Saskatoon

J ack McLeod might not be a household name in hockey, but
he's done it all and continues to enjoy the game. McLeod plays
in the over-60 recreational league in Saskatoon, where, at age
74, he's sort of a middle-of-the-road player, the oldest active
player being Fred Dawes at 87, "and he's one of the most beauti-
ful skaters I've ever seen," said McLeod. "A lot of the guys played
hockey all through their lives. They never quit," he said.

In his case, he did walk away from playing for about 20 years,
while he focussed on flying a company jet out of Saskatoon. McLeod
said he still enjoys hitting the ice twice a week. "It's something to do.
We have a great time. I can hardly skate anymore, I need a knee
replaced, but I go out there. It's a good pastime," he said.

While McLeod continues to play hockey at an age when most
have hung up their skates years ago, he may in a sense be making
up for lost time as a youth. He grew up in the tiny community
of Hazlet, Saskatchewan, where the amenities of hockey just did
not exist. "We never had a rink. We skated on frozen sloughs and
the dam west of town," he said. The absence of a rink meant he

never played organized hockey as a youth. "Not at all. I think the population, the highest it ever got was 100, maybe 99," he said, suggesting there were simply not enough kids to make up teams. "We used to play one game (a) year. We'd go to Cabri, 21 miles north of us. We would go in the spring and play if the ice hadn't melted." Relying on sloughs meant having to wait until freeze-up for ice to start with. When it became extremely cold, the ice would crack so badly skating was nearly impossible, pushing the kids off skates. "We played a lot of road hockey," he said.

So while McLeod knew how to skate, it wasn't until he turned 13 and headed to Notre Dame at Wilcox that he started hockey in an organized way. He attended the fabled institute at a time when its founder, Athol Murray, was still in charge. "Everybody knew Pére, he was just one of the guys. He was a good guy. He was fairly strict, but he had to be in a college like that," said McLeod. The stay at Notre Dame was short, and he moved on to the Moose Jaw Canucks, who were in the Saskatchewan Junior Hockey League at the time. There, McLeod honed his hockey skills to the point that, as a 19-year-old, 5-foot-9, 165-pound right winger, he signed a professional hockey contract with the New York Rangers. He joined the National Hockey League team in the fall of 1949.

New York was a long way away in more than distance from Hazlet, or Wilcox, or even Moose Jaw. "It was a kind of a culture shock, I tell you that," said McLeod. On the ice it was also an adjustment, one not made any easier by the realities of the times. "In those days there was hardly any coaching," said McLeod. As a result, he never really learned how to take the bumps and bashes he would encounter in the rugged NHL. "I did get injured quite a bit," he said. "I wish I'd had a little more coaching to learn how to look after myself. There was more open ice hitting back then. If they caught you with your head down you were in for bad luck."

It didn't help that McLeod's role quickly evolved into checking the opposition's top line. He recalled the words of his coach, "Kid, I don't care if you ever score a goal, just make sure your winger don't score a goal." At the time, that meant lining up against players such as Gordie Howe, Maurice Richard, Elmer Lach, Sid Abel, and a host of other snipers. "The nights sometimes got pretty long, I tell you," said McLeod. There was some good news in New York, too. "In the spring of '50, we went to the Stanley Cup finals against Detroit," said McLeod. "We lost in the seventh game in the third overtime."

At the time, hockey didn't have the highest of profiles in New York, and the Rangers were forced out of Madison Square Gardens during the finals to make way for the circus. They played their home games in Toronto. He still believes that, had they had the benefit of home ice, his name might well be engraved on the Cup. It would be as close as McLeod would come. His NHL career would span only 106 games. He scored 14 goals and added 23 assists for 37 points from his checking role. By the start of the 1955–56 season, he was back in Saskatchewan playing with the Saskatoon Quakers of the old Western Hockey League. He had a chance to play in the American Hockey League, but figured if it wasn't the NHL, he might as well be back home. The WHL would be home for most of his career, and he played not only for the Quakers, but the Vancouver Canucks and the Calgary Stampeders, before retiring in 1960.

While retirement often means the end of one's story on the ice, for McLeod it was a sort of beginning. He was living in Swift Current after retiring, working, with his son in school. Hockey seemed a thing of the past. "Then right around Christmas that year, the (Trail) Smoke Eaters called," said McLeod. "They said they wanted me to play for them. I hadn't even been on the ice." So McLeod borrowed a pair of skates (Calgary had kept his last professional pair when he retired) and headed to the Swift

Current rink for a skate. He knew he was not in game shape, but he accepted the offer, knowing Trail would represent Canada at the World Hockey Championships in 1961. "I got on the train and went out to Trail. They gave me a new pair of skates when I got there and I played that night," said McLeod. He didn't have a good game. The Smoke Eaters were heading out on the road, a touring exhibition in preparation for the World Championships. McLeod's next game was in the familiar confines of the Moose Jaw rink, but his play didn't improve. It was so bad, the team's management suggested maybe he wasn't ready for what was to come. "I knew I could play on the team once I got in shape," said McLeod. So he made the Smoke Eaters a deal—if he didn't lead the team in scoring through the exhibition games, he'd buy his own airplane ticket home. In his next game—only his third with the team—he had "three or four goals and a couple of assists," in a game in Yorkton. From there he was back in the flow. "I did lead the team," he said with a chuckle.

Things got better for McLeod once the World Championships started in Switzerland—games were played in both Geneva and Lausanne. "I led the tournament in goals. I had 10 goals in six games and was the all-star right winger," he said. The Smoke Eaters also won the championship, the last senior team to capture it. It would be 31 years—1994—before another Canadian team earned the honour. It was obviously a career highlight for McLeod. "I think it would have to be. I really enjoyed that tournament. I had never played European hockey before. It was wide open, so I could really motor."

While he found more open ice, it didn't mean the European teams didn't know how to hit. It took until the famed 1972 Canada-Russia Summit Series before many Canadians appreciated how good teams like the Russians were. With a World Championship on the resume, McLeod returned home to life without hockey, until in 1968 an offer came he couldn't refuse. Through Father Murray at Notre Dame, an offer came from Father David Bauer to coach the Canadian national team. McLeod accepted and enjoyed the role, especially the conversations with the likes of the famous Russian coach Anatoli Tarasov, whom most look at as the father of Russian hockey. "He never spoke English to the media, but between him and me we'd communicate quite easily," said McLeod.

McLeod's time with the national team included coaching at the 1968 Olympic Games in Grenoble. Canada earned bronze, while Russia took home the gold and Czechoslovakia the silver. "It was a great experience," he said, adding that in that era, the Canadian team at the Olympics was not as high-profile an event as it is today. "I don't think the people in Canada knew we were even over there, to tell the truth." The results were about what was expected. "We had a young team, but it was just the opportunity to play in the Olympics for everybody," he said. The Russians were the class of the event and a loss to them stopped Canada's chances of a better finish. "We went into it wanting nothing but the gold. Against the Russians, we got down a couple of goals, and you get down a couple of goals to them, it was pretty tough sledding." McLeod said the national team worked hard throughout his tenure as coach, "but weren't quite as talented" as European teams in an era before the top players from those countries headed to the NHL.

After a stint with the national team as coach, McLeod's career would once more return to Saskatoon, where he would spend six seasons as head coach of the WHL Blades. His best season was 1975–76, when he guided the Blades to a 43–19–10 record and a winning percentage of .667. McLeod's last season with the team was 1978–79.

It was a long road from Hazlet to New York to the World Hockey Championships to old-timer hockey in Saskatoon, but

McLeod said he has enjoyed every facet of his long association with the sport. In 1999, McLeod's career was marked by induction into the International Ice Hockey Federation's Hall of Fame, joining the likes of Wayne Gretzky, Father David Bauer, and his old coaching friend, Anatoli Tarasov. The IIHF created the Hall of Fame in Zurich, Switzerland, in 1997 to honour players, officials, and builders who have made valuable contributions to the game internationally. "I was pretty happy about that," he said of the induction. "I appreciate it. It was nice to get the recognition."

A Step Taken into History

Fred Sasakamoose may have played only 11 games in the National Hockey League, but they were historic games nevertheless. When Sasakamoose first stepped onto the ice as a member of the Chicago Blackhawks in 1954, it marked the first time a native player had made the NHL. "It was a shock when I went to that dressing room," said Sasakamoose, who joined the Hawks for a game in Toronto's Maple Leaf Gardens after completing his final junior year with Moose Jaw. "I sat down and looked around and saw players like Bill Mosienko and Max Bentley ... Now that was something I'll never forget."

Sasakamoose said he recalls being called over to the penalty box that first night during warm-ups. It was Foster Hewitt, the voice of the Hockey Night In Canada radio broadcasts. "He wanted to know how to pronounce my name—is it Saskatoon-moose or Saskatchewan-moose?" he said with a chuckle. And when the game started, the packed Gardens were almost intimidating to a 19-year-old. "I don't really know how it felt," admitted Sasakamoose. After the game it was on to Chicago and another moment for memories. Sasakamoose said the old Chicago Stadium was famous for its organ. "As soon as I stepped on the ice he played the Indian Love Call."

Over the next 10 games, Sasakamoose would play in every historic rink in the then-six-team NHL. However, the 'Hawks failed to make the playoffs, so it was back to Saskatchewan for Sasakamoose. On his way to his family's home near Debden, he stopped in Humboldt, where he ended up buying a new car "with lots of chrome" for $3,900. With his new car, Sasakamoose slowly traversed some seven miles of trail to Debden. "There was no highway, just a little wagon trail," he said. "I stopped in front of the old log house. It was only 20 by 25, one room, no power, no running water, no bathroom." There, Sasakamoose sat in his new car, waiting for his mother to emerge from the tiny house to surprise her. "You should have heard my mother when I got out of the car," he said. Even now as he talks of it, "I break down a little bit," the quiver evident in his voice.

The tiny log house was a long way from Chicago. In fact, as the two worlds were so far apart, Sasakamoose made the decision not to go back to the NHL. "A lot of people asked me why. They ask me if I was to start over, would I do it differently?" he said. "I said no, I enjoy who I am, where I'm at. Had I stayed in the big time, I probably would never have come home again, never seen my friends again." For Sasakamoose family is something he cherishes—maybe more than many, because as a child that part of his life was taken away from him. Sasakamoose was born on the Sandy Lake Reserve and learned to skate at a young age. "They were what you called bobskates. My grandfather used to tie them to my moccasins when I was six years old," he said. His grandfather would also take him to the slough to water the horses and to fish. "He made a little rink, 10 by 10, where I could skate. Sometimes

Grandfather would get sort of upset. He'd say he wasn't getting any bites because I was making too much noise playing."

Then family life came to an end. At the age of seven, Sasakamoose was taken away from his family to the St. Michael's Residential School at Duck Lake. There was hockey at the school, but Sasakamoose said, "You had to earn your skates." That was done by milking cows, doing other jobs, or, as he did, giving up ice cream treats to another kid to get an old pair of skates when he was 12. While there was hockey, most of the experiences at the residential school were not good. "I was only seven years old when I was loaded into that truck—that three-ton truck," he said, at a Gathering of Residential Survivors conference in Yorkton. They are memories that will never leave Sasakamoose. "Sometimes I wonder as I look back a little bit … There was a lot of heartache in those schools, we all know that," he said.

Attending the school was not a matter of choice, but of government policy. And so his mother cried as Sasakamoose was taken away, and life took a turn to the dark side. There was a time he believed "this thing was being forgotten and left behind me." But now Sasakamoose finds himself sharing his story as people try to come to terms with what happened in the residential schools more than a half-century ago, although the wounds are still being felt in generations now. The federal government has even begun offering compensation to survivors, but Sasakamoose questions what they think dollars will do. "What am I going to get compensated for? It was done. It completely killed me," he said. "Nine years I went through that system." During those years he was supposed to be educated, but school amounted to only two hours a day. "The rest of the time I had to do chores," he said. He emerged with only a Grade 6 education. So he milked cows and separated cream, only to watch as he and his schoolmates received a ration of skimmed milk. "The priests got the cream and the butter and the pies," he said.

But the failure to get a good education was not the only effect of the residential school that has left scars on Sasakamoose and others. "I never saw my parents," he said. "I never knew my parents." By regulation, parents were not allowed to visit their children at the schools. "It was against the laws and the policy," he said. And visits home were short-lived and rare. "I didn't even see my sister and she lived next door," added Sasakamoose, whose four brothers and sister were all taken to St. Michael's School. And the loss of family was only the beginning for Sasakamoose, who admitted, "Sometimes we struggle to talk about these things." But he also realizes that the stories must come out and be shared. "If we are going to heal … everything we went through in our lives must come out, if we want to heal together," he said.

And so he tells a little of the school. "I've seen kids in there sexually abused … so darned bad that I couldn't even face them," he said. Sasakamoose said that the knowledge of the abuse stayed with him to the point that, even meeting those people today, he finds it difficult to look them in the eyes. "But we were small. We couldn't do anything," he said. "If we did do something we were severely punished." And their culture, too, was stripped away from the native students. "Our language was taken away. We couldn't talk Cree. It was just taken away from us," said Sasakamoose. Even today he struggles for answers to the past. "I talk to my Creator," he said. "I leave my home and go to the hill, and I worship. I take my sweetgrass and I pray for forgiveness."

Yet, while the abuse and hardship swirled around Sasakamoose, there was a place he found that he could excel in spite of the realities he faced. That was on the ice. In the 1947–48 hockey season, a team from school would win the midget championship. "We were the best," said Sasakamoose with obvious pride. But even in that he faced the reality that he was an Indian in a society run by whites. Short of players, the team picked up two white players from an orphanage in Prince Albert. Although teammates, "they (the Oblate priests) segregated us from the white kids," said Sasakamoose at the Yorkton Conference. "It was so bad the white players ate with the priests, receiving better food than the rest of the team, who sat at a separate table," he said. "I don't know why … we played as a team. To play as a team you've got to stay together. The only time we could talk to them was in the dressing room." Still, Sasakamoose said he realizes now the provincial title was an accomplishment, considering there were only about 150 kids at the school, ranging in age from about five to 14, so there were not a lot of options when picking a team.

Sasakamoose said he does recognize the school taught him one thing that has been beneficial through his life. "There was a lot of discipline. I think that was a key part of my life," he said. "The priests didn't allow you to say no." However, Sasakamoose wasn't thinking about the discipline of hockey after the provincial title. He just wanted to go home. "After nine years in residential school, not seeing my parents for any length of time, I just wanted to go home. I was lonely," he said.

However, the stay at home would be short-lived. "I was working out in the field stooking grain for these farmers when I saw a car on the road allowance," said Sasakamoose. When the car stopped, he could see Father Roselle from the school emerge. He said he was scared they were coming to take him away again, so he tried to get away. The priest and another man came to talk to Sasakamoose's parents. The other man was George Vogen of the Moose Jaw Canucks, a junior team who wanted the young player to join them. "I said, 'I'm not going. I've been away nine years. I don't want to leave again.' I had hardly heard of Moose Jaw," he said. "I cried. I didn't want to go. I didn't want to leave Mom." But

Vogen convinced Sasakamoose and his family, and he headed south. "I'd never been to the outside world before—to the white man's world."

Sasakamoose said that without Vogen's support, he likely wouldn't have stayed in Moose Jaw, or hockey. "This man had determination. He wanted me so bad … He would do anything for me. I could tell he cared. He had a dream for me. I know that now." It wasn't easy in Moose Jaw, at least to start. "I sat in the corner of the dressing room," said Sasakamoose. "I didn't want to lift my head up. I was ashamed and I was scared." After two weeks, Sasakamoose tried to hitch home, but Vogen found him in Chamberlin and convinced him to stick it out.

Along the way, Sasakamoose credited NHLer George Hunchuk with helping him develop. The pair met one day when the young player snuck into the rink where Hunchuk was skating. "I watched him for about 20 minutes," said Sasakamoose. Eventually, Hunchuk skated up to him. "He said, 'Chief, would you like to skate like me?' I admired the way he skated. He just floated on the ice." The two met the next day and Sasakamoose began to learn, although he said even as he tried to sleep, he was learning. "That night when I went to bed, every time I closed my eyes I saw him. I studied his movements." By his fourth year with the Canucks, he was named Most Valuable Player, and during a game in Edmonton the Hobbema tribe bestowed the title "Chief Running Deer" on him. There was a circle of chiefs on the ice and Sasakamoose knelt down and they placed a war bonnet on him, and bestowed the title. "That was a thrill. I was being recognized by the Indian nation at that time."

But a bigger thrill was coming. The season in Moose Jaw ended and the team felt the sadness of another year without a championship. "George Vogel came in. Our heads were down because we were beat out in the playoffs." That was when he read a telegram telling Sasakamoose to meet the Blackhawks in Toronto. "You couldn't go any higher. You've touched the ceiling ... That was a wonderful feeling, one of the best feelings I've ever had." Sasakamoose would not record a goal or an assist in the NHL. He would spend a few games in the minors, but soon chose to return to his wife and give up on professional hockey. "I've had a good, decent life. I never had money, but I had my family. That's my riches," he said. He has nine children, 39 grandchildren, and 18 great-grandchildren. "We have had a happy life."

Red Baron Remembered
for Double Hat Trick

A single night in Philadelphia carved a place in hockey history for Gordon "Red" Berenson. Berenson was in his first full season, 1968–69, with the St. Louis Blues when he became only the second player in National Hockey League history to score six goals. He was the first to score a double hat trick in a road game. Syd Howe had managed the feat in 1944 with Detroit, but on home ice. In Berenson's case, he scored every goal in even situations, adding to the mystique of the performance. After two periods, the Blues were up 5–0 in the game, with Berenson potting all five. "You play long enough, you've got to have a good game once in a while," said Berenson with a chuckle. "It was just one of those nights when everything went in."

While the performance is obviously historic, Berenson doesn't hold it at the top of his own list. "I'm surprised nobody else has done it," he said, adding, "I think I've played better games, but just didn't get the goals." Still, the memory is there. "I broke my stick after the fifth goal. I got another one, and it felt like a club," he said. But, he took a shot, and it felt great, and the puck found the twine over the shoulder of goaltender, Doug Favell, for the sixth goal. "And I had a post and a crossbar in 10 shots," he said with a laugh. This was only one game in a solid NHL career, followed by an equally good run as a coach.

Berenson said it all started with his roots in Regina. "Growing up in Regina, we played in the Regina Parks League," he said. "They had all the outdoor rinks flooded and organized. I thought it was a terrific league for average kids." The time on the outdoor rinks was a special one Berenson said he simply loved. "I think it was terrific," he said, adding, "We didn't know any better." Certainly his days as a young player were different from the well-heated rinks of today. "Television didn't come to Regina until about 1954. There were no computers or video games," he said. "The main entertainment was the rinks. The only thing to do was play outdoors. The outdoor hockey was a great opportunity. We probably had more ice time on a weekend than they do in a week, or maybe a month now."

In Berenson's case, though, he proved just a cut or two above the average, and he was soon playing with the Regina Patricias of the Saskatchewan Junior Hockey League. "When I got to be a junior hockey player it was a big step," he said. A big step, perhaps, but one he made with some ease, scoring 46 goals and 49 assists in his second season with the Patricias. In fact, when it comes to career highlights, Berenson said he rates playing with the Patricias in the "old stadium" at the top of his list. At the time, young prospects were usually snapped up by one of the six NHL franchises, and Berenson was the property of the Montreal Canadiens. However, the young forward had his own ideas of how to best develop as a player, making the move to the University of Michigan as his next step in hockey. That was for the start of the 1959–60 season, an era when few Saskatchewan players were heading to American college hockey. "It wasn't like this was brand new. There had been some players in Regina going off to college," said Berenson, pointing to players such as Red Hay, who went to Colorado College in 1956.

The choice of an American college wasn't particularly popular with the Canadiens, or his old team. "There were some bad feelings with the Pats," he said, adding that he had two years of junior eligibility left, but headed south because he had completed high school. It was a move he still looks back on as a key one in his career. "I think it really helped me develop as a player, and as a person," he said. It also helped fire him up for more, as he had an opportunity to watch Montreal whenever they played Detroit.

Still, the move to the U of M was something of a risk. At the time, only a handful of players were making the jump to the NHL from American colleges. "It (the college game) didn't have a good reputation," said Berenson, adding that the game has come a long, long way in quality. But even then there was talent at the college level. "There were a few players who could have played in the NHL if they had gotten a chance," said Berenson. "Or if they had been willing to make the sacrifices." The trickle to make the jump was starting, including the likes of Lou Angotti and Tony Esposito, and after three college seasons Berenson was on his way, too. "The wheel was starting to turn," he said.

Berenson, of course, signed with the fabled Canadiens, seeing action in his first full professional season before being shipped down to Hull-Ottawa of the EPHL. "I was pretty lucky," he said, noting that the old six-team NHL was tough to crack, and Montreal was maybe the toughest of the six. "You definitely had to pay your dues. Montreal was really old school. There really (weren't) a lot of opportunities."

The first game as a Canadien also rates highly for Berenson. "Just sitting in the Montreal dressing room, putting that sweater on was so satisfying," he said. Berenson remained focussed on making it in the NHL. "Like a lot of players I thought I could play, but just needed a chance," he said. For many players, including Berenson, the chance to play arrived in 1967, as the NHL doubled in size, adding six expansion franchises. By then Berenson was with the New York Rangers, but was moved to the fledgling St. Louis Blues. "I was going to a team where I had a chance to be a good player," he said. It also reunited him with then-Blues coach Scotty Bowman, who had coached him in the minors at Hull-Ottawa. "He (Bowman) thought I could play. He believed in me, and somewhere along the way, you have to have somebody believe in you," said Berenson. The Blues were the cream of the expansion crop in the early years, and Berenson credited Lynn Patrick and Bowman with building a veteran team through the expansion draft, including goaltender Glenn Hall, a fellow Saskatchewan product.

Berenson would spend nearly seven seasons as a Blue, time split by a five-season stint in Detroit. When he retired in 1978, he was just short of 1,000 career games at 987, with 261 goals and 397 assists. However, two of Berenson's most memorable games as an NHLer do not show up on the career list. He played two games with Team Canada in the fabled 1972 series against the Russians. "We really didn't realize it was going to be the historic series it was," said the only Saskatchewan-born player on the roster. "It really was. We didn't realize the impact it was having back in Canada." The team was in Sweden more than a week prior to the games in Russia, where they lost game five, but came back to win the final three games. "It was a hockey experience, but it was taking on greater significance than that," said Berenson. "It was a cultural experience, and a political experience." While the series win galvanized a nation, Berenson said it also taught lessons to the Canadian participants. "We really came to appreciate what we had back in North America, the quality of life we have, the freedoms we have," he said.

With his career complete in 1978, Berenson backed into a new career, assuming an assistant coaching role with the Blues. "I had no interest in coaching," he said. But St. Louis general manager Emile Francis, another Saskatchewan alumnus, had other ideas, asking the veteran to help head coach Barclay Plager. "I agreed to do it just so I wouldn't have to move again," he said with a chuckle. When Plager became ill, Berenson took over the top job. In 1980–'81 the Blues under Berenson recorded 107 points, earning him the Jack Adams Award as the NHL's top coach. It was the first unanimous choice in the award's history.

"It was a good experience," said Berenson, who would coach in Buffalo as well, before returning to his old alma mater. "I could have stayed in the NHL. I was comfortable there. I knew the culture in the NHL." But "I always had a soft spot in my heart for Michigan. I've really enjoyed the college coaching experience. I really believe in kids going to school. The worst thing they get out of it is an education." In 1996, Berenson led the Wolverines to a national title, their first since 1964.

Berenson has seen a number of players advance from his program to the NHL, such as Brendan Morrison, Marty Turco, and Mike Comrie. "You just knew they were going to play. It was just a matter of time," he said. "Some kids just have something inside them that makes them succeed." As a coach, Berenson said he expects dedication to bring out the best in young players. "I'm never really satisfied because I'm always pushing them to the next level," he said. "I'm a tough coach to play for in that regard. I always want them to get better."

But maybe not even today's college hockey can provide better memories than Berenson's fondly remembered hockey days in Regina. "That was the start of everything. I still look back on that time," he said, pointing to an outdoor rink at Connaught Street and 8th Avenue in Regina, where they went to play even in snow-storms. "I'd shovel the whole rink off by myself if I had to. Even in a blizzard, we still wanted to play." And while he has lived in Michigan for years, Saskatchewan is still home. "We still call it home. We just haven't been there a lot," he said. "My roots are still going to be in Saskatchewan."

It Was "Hammer" Time in Philly

Dave Schultz's nickname pretty well sums up his style on the ice. He was simply known as "The Hammer." Schultz earned his way into the National Hockey League through a willingness to drop the gloves and roll up the penalty minutes. In 535 regular-season games in the big show, he amassed 2,294 minutes in the sin bin. It's a style Schultz, who played through the 1970s, makes no apology for. "Why do they downplay, downplay, downplay fighting?" he asked emphatically. "It is as unique as scoring. The fans love it just as much, if not more." Schultz goes further in suggesting that fighting needs to be part of hockey, something which is missing in the game of the 2000s, and it's hurting hockey at the NHL level. "When somebody gives a cheap shot to somebody, they should have to pay for it," said Schultz, suggesting that doesn't mean a couple of days off through a league-imposed suspension. "Let the players police themselves."

With the current instigator rule, the policing on the ice is impeded. "The instigator rule doesn't work," said Schultz, adding that, because of the rules, he finds today's NHL difficult to watch. "Guys will give a cheap shot and never have to pay for it." Schultz said fights are a way to put some discipline into the game without the injuries that can occur with cheap shots and stick work. "Nobody ever gets hurt in a fist fight—maybe feelings a few times."

Schultz, of course, came to NHL prominence with a team noted for its toughness. The Philadelphia Flyers of the era were noted as the "Broadstreet Bullies." The team included the likes of Bob "Battleship" Kelly, André "Moose" Dupont, Don "Big Bird" Saleski, another Saskatchewan alumnus, and of course, "The Hammer." "We were the 'Broadstreet Bullies' and I did as much as anybody in creating that," said Schultz.

There isn't much room to argue with the success the Flyers had. In 1974, the team won its first ever Stanley Cup, capturing it again a season later, and going to the finals in 1976, before losing to the Montreal Canadiens. Through it all, Schultz took a pretty regular shift and gained a notoriety that still lingers. "To this day it's beyond me. A lot of it was just hype, and we did win two championships, which made a major difference, but I'm better known today than I was even 10 years ago." Not bad for a guy who was born in the small community of Waldheim, Saskatchewan, and who moved around to a number of other small Saskatchewan towns during his youth as his mechanic-father moved for employment. With each move, one thing stayed constant for Schultz and his brother Ray, who died a number of years ago—their love of hockey. Ray made it to the minor pros himself, playing with the Syracuse Blazers and Philadelphia Firebirds, among four teams in the 1970s. Dave added that his brother was also on the set for the filming of the hockey cult-classic *Slapshot*, but never made it into a scene that made the final cut.

The earliest lessons came living on a farm near Cater,

Saskatchewan. "I started skating out in front of the house on the dugout," he said, adding that it was the start of an intense love affair with the game as a youth. "My brother and I were rink rats forever." Time spent in Medstead was punctuated by hours of public skating on the community's outdoor rink. It was the same everywhere the family moved. "Hockey, that's all we did, all we really cared about, me and my brother," he said. "It would be 20, 30, 40 below, but there was this little hut with a wood stove, and we went and skated. We played street hockey. We played on the pond. That's all I cared about."

When the family moved back to Waldheim, the hospital where Schultz had been the first baby born had already closed, and the family moved into the building's basement as an apartment. "We left tons of puck marks in those long hallways." Two years in Lucky Lake are fondly recalled as a time hockey skills progressed. "I played a couple of years there. There were very few people, so I had two good years of development ... I would play defence as a bantam, and right after that play midget as a forward. It was a good development year. There wasn't much else to do. We didn't even have a gym at the school."

Beyond the games, life always revolved around the game. When in Waldheim, Schultz and his brother were helpers with the local senior team. "We were the guys pushing the scrapers around to clean the ice between periods." Schultz also recalled one hometown rink that had no room behind the boards for a goal judge to sit. "I used to stand on top of the net right on the ice. I never got hit, either," he said. All the games in all the small rinks paid off when Schultz was picked up by the Estevan Bruins, playing as a rogue team at the time, outside recognized amateur hockey. He was cut and drifted to Swift Current, which was just launching the Broncos. It was a rough and tumble game, and one Schultz said he actually shied away from. "I was afraid to fight. I was intimidated half of the time. If I wasn't on the bench (when trouble started) I ended up there," he said. "I was still a feisty kind of player, but I'd go into the corner and give it to some guy in the face with my glove, and then get out of there."

While not yet the physical presence he would become, Schultz was scoring in the neighbourhood of 35 goals and a similar number of assists with the Broncos, enough to attract the attention of the NHL Flyers. It probably helped that in his final year of junior he headed out east to play a half-season in Quebec, going to the final against the Montreal Junior Canadiens, who won the series, and moving on to defeat the Regina Pats in the '69 Memorial Cup final. That same spring, Schultz was drafted in the fifth round, 52nd overall, by Philadelphia.

"I knew I had some potential. Certainly I was hoping to be drafted. I had my high school, but really had never thought about going to college," he said. As a professional, Schultz's first stop was the Salem Rebels in the Eastern Hockey League. It was a decision that made the player. In his first game he had a fight, and before the season was over, he had 356 penalty minutes and a respectable 32 goals. The fans embraced him with the nickname "Sgt. Schultz," and fate was set in motion. "It was an animal league. You go around a defenceman you'd get a two-hander, or a spear. After that, I always had more than 300 PIMs," he said.

Never really enjoying the fighting, Schultz said he appreciated that teammates and fans liked his efforts with the mitts. "I thought about it a lot, and I got pretty good at it. That was my role. It was the whole thing for the next 11 years." It was never a case of being told to throw punches, but Schultz said players knew their roles, adding that no one could be forced to fight. "You had to be willing to do it. Some guys liked it. I didn't, but I did it."

The following season, Schultz was with the Quebec Aces of the American Hockey League, the team's last season. It was a year where the junior Ramparts were drawing 10,000 to a game in the Quebec capital led by Guy Lafleur, while the Aces played to only a couple of thousand. The penalty minutes rose to 382.

In Richmond the next year, the sin bin time rose to 392. Schultz said his fights were featured news in the Virginia city. He recalled a game with Providence. Before the game, everybody knew he and future teammate André Dupont would fight. "They knew we were going to go at it that night, so they marketed it in the newspaper."

At the end of the season, Schultz left behind the minors, joining the Flyers for the start of the 1972–73 season. His first fight, a few games into the season, would be against an eventual friend, Keith Magnuson (also from Saskatchewan), who toiled with Chicago. As for the toughest opponent in all the years of fighting in the NHL, Schulz says there were many tough guys, but he gives the nod to Boston Bruin Terry O'Reilley, with whom he dropped the gloves "about 10 times." "It wasn't a matter of how tough you were. It was if you were willing to go every time," he said. The die was cast, and Schultz starred as a Flyer at a time when the team was known for its physical style and feared by many on the ice. Even the famous Russian Red Army team skated off the ice during a 1976 game at the Philadelphia Spectrum, when they didn't like the check from Ed Van Imp, yet another Saskatchewan player with the Flyers. "The league said, 'Play your game,'" said Schultz. "Sure, we were playing a little tough. We were trying to intimidate them a little bit. But, were we hitting them too hard? Give me a break."

It was a good ride in Philly, but after the Stanley Cup loss to Montreal in the spring of 1976, Schultz's career with the Flyers came to an end. He was traded to Los Angeles, a season later to Pittsburgh, and yet another year later to Buffalo. He would retire in 1980. While he said the trade treadmill was disappointing at the end of his career, there are no regrets. "I've stated emphatically I've been blessed in many ways. It's been quite exciting," he said, adding that he credits two things, growing up in Saskatchewan and playing hockey. "It's been quite a ride."

Personal Tragedy Turns into Golden Moment

When Kelly Downes accepted his world championship gold medal in the spring of 2004, it was something he admitted he had never dreamed of. Downes earned the medal with the Canadian Standing Upright Amputee team, which went undefeated through five games at the championships in Prague. "They were beyond anything I expected. We beat the hell out of everybody," said Downes. The championships in Prague were the second World Championships; Canada won the first edition in 2003 in Helsinki, Finland.

The winning goaltender on the 2003 team retired, and the back-up from 2003 did not make the 2004 edition. Downes said the situation added pressure on him. "I don't want to be the new guy the coach picked and then not win gold. But what better challenge than 'go and win the gold'?" And win they did. In four games through the round robin portion of the tournament, the Canadians allowed only one goal, that getting past Downes in a game against Finland. "I can't remember his name but he played in the World Junior Championships with Teemu Selanne (a long-time National Hockey League veteran). He lost his left hand to cancer, but he's a good hockey player. It kind of sucked to let one sneak by, but he scored half the goals for Finland."

Downes split time in each of the round robin games against Finland, the United States, the Czech Republic, and Russia with goaltending tandem mate Mike Cleavley. The top two teams in the round robin—the Canadians and Americans—met for the gold, with Downes sitting on the bench as Cleavley backstopped the team to the win. "That was a really tough pill to swallow," admitted Downes, although the bad feeling evaporated with the presentation of the medals. "I don't know if words can describe that. It was wonderful," he said. The team made the moment even more memorable. "Instead of having the national anthem played, we all sang it at the top of our lungs."

Being a member of a Canadian national team was never something Downes expected, even though he, like most young-sters in Saskatchewan, had a love of hockey. From about the age of five, he was a hockey player. "I went between the pipes at about seven," he said. "At that age every kid gets to try it, and when the coach put me in I just loved it." Downes admitted that goaltending can at times be a lonely place, but also one where the goaltender can win or lose a game on his own efforts. The young Regina net-minder stayed in hockey until he was 16, when he soured on the game. "There was one bad season, with terrible coaches. I think we might have won one game all year. It just broke my spirit. I just couldn't deal with it. I was mad going to the rink and I never felt that way before … so I just hung them up." However, it's hard to completely turn one's back on a love, and by the time Downes turned 20, he realized he had to get back on the ice. "I went and bought equipment, and never looked back." The hockey was only at the recreational level, but that was enough for Downes. "That was enough for me to realize I love the game more than anything else again. I'd forgot how much I loved it."

For Downes, hockey is something that is great on the ice, but it goes beyond a game, too. "Playing the game itself is just unbelievable, but another part is just sitting in the dressing room and talking about the game." Teammates at the rec level might not be best friends off the ice, but come game night, Downes said, "We meet up at the game, and would do anything for each other." For Downes, finding his way back to hockey was fulfilling, something he enjoyed while attending classes in Humboldt, and when he moved to Melfort for work, his hockey gear went with him.

But Downes' hockey and his life were in for a massive change when, on March 20, 2002, he suffered an on-the-job accident. He was welding on a cultivator when a wing fell. Diving out of the way, he almost avoided the crashing piece of equipment, all but his right foot. Half his foot was caught and crushed. Initially doctors were confident the foot could be repaired. "They were fighting to save it," said Downes. An initial operation was undertaken. Then a toe died and had to be removed, followed by a second. "They were taking toes off as I watched them die." In the end, doctors realized the damage was too great, and actually awoke Downes out of his third surgery to tell him they felt it was time to amputate. The announcement was not a total shock. "I had a really great team of doctors, and they said not to worry, but it was in the back of my head." In the end, Downes accepted the doctors' decision to amputate half of his foot. "I told them, 'You're the boss. If you feel that is the best thing, go ahead and do it.' I made my peace with it after about four hours of crying my eyes out."

However, after the operation to remove a large portion of his foot, Downes admitted he couldn't look at it for four days. After having a pin removed, Downes started on his rehabilitation, a process that was arduous, as he had to learn how to walk all over again. "I couldn't even balance on my right leg for five seconds." However, the goaltender had something else in mind, too, a return to the ice. Just five months after getting his prosthesis, he skated. "That's how much I wanted to play." Downes said hockey was never far from his mind, even as the doctors talked of amputation. "That was the first question out of my mouth: 'Would I be able to play hockey again?'" The answer became his inspiration. "The doctor said, 'If you want to.'" However, Downes said initially as he started physiotherapy, he considered selling his equipment. But his therapist Lisa Morrison talked him out of it. Through hard work, Downes would get back on the ice, but quickly found his size 12 skates didn't work well on only half a foot. "I couldn't stop. I couldn't turn." Then he donned a size 8 skate on his right foot, and he was away again. "When I stepped on the ice with that size eight, I just knew I was going to be able to play again." However, it wasn't an easy road. "There was lots of pain, lots of tears, but the drive was there because I just love the game so much." By February 2003, less than a year after the accident, Downes was back in goal in a game situation. "I couldn't stop smiling. It was different, too, because I was still teaching myself new things." The game was also a benchmark for Downes. "It was a defining moment, that I wasn't going to let this beat me."

Then the world on the Internet opened a door to an opportunity for Downes. "I was just surfing the Internet for stuff on amputee sports," he recalled. The search led him to a page on the Canadian Standing Upright Amputee team. He emailed the team's general manager and found that amputee goaltenders "are very few and far between." Downes was invited to a tryout camp in Toronto in November 2003, with four other goaltenders and 22 skaters. The team that emerged, including Downes as one of the two netminders, included a broad range of amputees. The other goaltender had lost his glove hand. Some players had lost arms and legs, and it is common to see amputations ranging from thigh to foot. But the goal remains the same, lifting the awareness of the sport to the level where it has Canadian government support. That will mean having at least seven countries playing in order to be sanctioned. So far only Canada, the United States, Russia, Czechoslovakia, and Finland attend the World Championship, but Japan and Germany are looking at fielding teams, said Downes.

As it stands, though, Downes is the lone Saskatchewan player on the team, which he said is a matter of pride. "I'm very proud to be representing our province in a game I love." It's a pride Downes said he plans to keep focussed by continuing with the Canadian Standing Upright Amputee team. "My goalie coach said this should be my job for the next 10 years if I come to camp every year healthy and stronger."

The World Championships are only planned for every second year, but Downes said a sort of challenge series against the U.S. will be held in Calgary in 2005. "We've got to stay together as a team." The longer-term goal is to demonstrate the sport at the 2006 Winter Olympics in Italy, and have it a full medal sport by 2010 in Vancouver. Beyond the play on the ice, Downes said hockey has helped him come to terms with his lost foot. "That's my fairy tale. I never knew if I was even going to skate again and then to have a gold medal dream and then realize it is amazing," he said. "I've come a long way in two years. I take a lot of pride in that."

A Saskatchewan First

U niversities across Canada have vied for a national crown for years, but only once has the championship come to a Saskatchewan team. The University of Saskatchewan Huskies had made it to the national final for two years in a row, coming up empty both times on late goals by the University of Moncton. But the Huskies were not to be denied in the 1982–83 season, this time facing Concordia in the final and coming away with the coveted championship via a 6–2 win.

The win was heartfelt for Willie Desjardins, a five-year Huskies team member who was the tournament's Most Valuable Player after setting a tournament record of 11 points in three games. "I enjoyed that victory. We had worked hard for it. You don't get that feeling very often. The harder you work for something the better it feels."

Tim Hodgson was born in Saskatoon and he said there was never any doubt he would one day attend the local university. Since he was a hockey player—he had being playing Junior B with the Saskatoon Quakers, who represented the province in the

Canada Winter Games one season—it was also natural to try out for the Huskies. Winning the Canadian title four seasons later was the cream on top of a career that in many ways was pre-conceived for Hodgson. "In my mind we were clearly the better team (in the final) and the score was an indication of that," he said. As for the feeling after the win, Hodgson said, "Euphoria certainly would describe it."

Dave Adolph was in his fifth year patrolling the Huskies' blue line and was wearing an assistant captain's patch when the team finally won the coveted title. However, he wasn't on the ice at the final buzzer, having suffered a concussion in the game's first period. "I was in the first aid room. I never even got the chance to celebrate (until later). I'm still upset about that … It was more of a case of satisfaction than celebration," he said. "It was a sense of accomplishment, of a job well-done." It was a job the team set for themselves at the beginning of the season, with players designing class schedules around hockey so as to focus on gaining the CIAU title, said Adolph, who was born in Swift Current. "The guys were on an absolute mission."

Desjardins—who turned to coaching after his playing days, most recently with Medicine Hat of the Western Hockey League—said it was certainly a team effort for the Huskies. "The key thing on that team was there was so many quality players, so many guys who were leaders." There was also a feeling of unfinished business lingering from the two previous seasons. In fact, the feeling that they were ready to take the final step was what lured Desjardins back for a fifth year. The two losses in previous years were obviously disappointing, as well as close contests, and he said one of his goals had always been a national title, so returning for a final shot was a natural decision. "That was a great year," he said. "For me it was a fun year. At the end of that game I more or less knew my career was over."

Adolph said he, too, returned for a fifth season with hockey in mind. He pointed out that in those days it was possible to achieve a four-year degree in four years, even with extra-curricular sport obligations, so five-year players were somewhat rare in the CIAU then, whereas today they are more prevalent. Adolph is well aware of university hockey since playing, having coached for 15 seasons, including 11 as head coach with the Huskies through 2004. "I was a high school teacher and absolutely loved it," he said, noting that he had no intention of coaching until his old Huskies coach Dave King got him a spot with Lethbridge as it started a hockey program. Now he looks at coaching as beyond a job. "It's more than a habit. It's a passion," he said. "I love everything about it." In his time with the Huskies, he has guided the team to five Canadian championship tournament berths, but has yet to capture one. "It's pretty frustrating, but like I said, it's tough to win," he said. It makes his one title as a player that much sweeter. "I still go to the national championships every year, even if my Huskies aren't in it, and they still talk about that (winning) team."

Although Desjardins would play one year of European hockey following the championship season, the game sort of put an exclamation point on a career that saw him leave his home in Climax at 14 to become something of a hockey gypsy, playing midget, the Saskatchewan Junior Hockey League, the Western Hockey League, and a year in Japan before joining the Huskies program.

Hodgson, also a team assistant captain, agreed that having been so close the previous two years made the eventual Canadian crown in some ways a more deeply appreciated victory. "Having been denied twice in the CIAU championships, and to finally win it that third year, it was special," he said. "We had all invested a lot of time, blood, sweat, and tears to get it."

The Huskies were a team that seemed to grow into its

championship. Desjardins recalled that in his first year with the team they managed a woeful 3–21 record. "It was a difficult year, but there were some really good people even on that team," he said. What was needed was some ingredient to get the good players winning hockey. Enter coach Dave King, who became one of the most respected coaches in the game. Adolph said King was proactive in going out and "finding quality Saskatchewan players and bringing them home," which quickly strengthened the Huskies' program. By the time they defeated Calgary, a powerhouse, on the way to their first national finals, the team was turning heads. "The first year (under King) it was tough, that's for sure, but after that it started to grow. Beating Calgary … I don't even think we were on the radar for most people at that point," he said.

King was certainly a motivator for the success, according to the team's captain. "He sort of helped us focus. He got us all on the same page, going the same way," said Desjardins. King was a coach who expected a lot from his team, but gave something back at the same time, and it was a successful formula for the Huskies. "He had a lot of real good qualities," said Desjardins. "He never asked you to do something he wouldn't do himself … He was demanding. He expected players to perform, but he was always prepared to help us achieve."

"Demanding" was also a word Hodgson used to describe King, but added that his arrival helped set the Huskies—perennial basement dwellers in their conference—on a path to the top. "Dave King came in and made changes because there had to be a change in direction," said Hodgson, who added that one change was King's innovative approach to game systems. For example, his approach to having players cycle the puck down low in the offensive zone was almost revolutionary at the time. "It was something that really wasn't in vogue at the time," said Hodgson. But it was an effective way to run things in the offensive zone. Adolph said

King's influence helped mold him as a coach, and he suspected Desjardins, too. "We all still use most of his methods. He was a fantastic technical coach. We were always well-prepared when we played."

Desjardins said one aspect of university hockey is that games are focussed on weekends, allowing plenty of preparation time. "A strength of university hockey is you have a week to prepare for whoever you are playing," he said, adding that he liked the pacing. "For me the schedule was really good because I always thought about the game a lot." Desjardin's study of the game might explain why he turned to coaching after his playing days, including the University of Calgary, five years in Japan, a season in Germany, and stops in the WHL. The prep work paid off in the championship final. "Moncton had beat us both the previous years and we fully expected to play them again in the final, but they didn't make it," said Desjardins. So instead of a familiar foe, the Huskies faced Concordia. "That's when the coaches and their preparation stuff came in," said Desjardins.

The other thing King brought to the struggling Huskies when he arrived was a change of thinking. "Dave brought a kind of attitude where we started expecting to win a little bit," said Desjardins. In the third year of making it to the championship tournament, Hodgson said the entire team had a different attitude. He recalled defeating Calgary in their first year heading to the finals to win the West. The win was really unexpected. "I don't think anybody would have expected we would make that much progress that year," he said. After defeating Calgary, the Huskies celebrated in a major way, looking at the western win as a huge victory.

By the third year of winning the West, there were a few handshakes, but no real celebration, because the team had its mind on a larger goal—the Canadian championship. "We had a different mental approach that third year. Our mindset was totally focussed on the championship," he said. Adolph agreed the mood was different. "I don't even remember celebrating," he said. The players were simply focussed on the games ahead. In the final, the feeling was positive from the outset, said Desjardins. "I remember we were all gathered around the goaltender (Bob Dugall) before the game, saying, 'Do you realize we'll be champions after this is over?'"

Hodgson, who would go on to play in Holland for one season, winning a championship there as well, called the CIAU crown the best moment of his hockey career. "It was a great feeling," he said. Hodgson reiterated that having to persevere over three years to achieve the goal made it that much more special.

Bad Season, Good Memories

It's a record that may well never be repeated in the Saskatchewan Junior Hockey League. And it's a record no one wants to even think about chasing. Yet there it sits—58 straight losses by the Regina Silver Foxes over the 1973–74 Saskatchewan Junior Hockey League season and into the 1974–75 season. Now, more than a quarter of a century later, the members of the squad look back on a season of defeat with surprisingly little remorse at the stack of losses they mounted as Silver Foxes—even though the team's 54 losses in the 1974–75 season, and the 545 goals they allowed that season, remain as an SJHL record. So do their two points, the lowest ever recorded in the league.

Phil Degenstein recalls joining the team partway through the season. "I played the last 20 games or so of the streak," said the former Silver Fox forward. You might think joining a team in the midst of weeks of repeated losses would have soured Degenstein on the move to the Silver Foxes, but that was not the case. Moving up from the ranks of Junior B hockey, Degenstein said it was still a move up, which was a positive. "I had friends on the team and it was still hockey out there," he said from his home in Regina. "We weren't totally outrageously bad." In fact, Degenstein said the line he was on, with Dave Desaultes and Marshall Hamilton, was pretty solid. "Our line, we could go out and get a couple (of goals)," he said. "There were still goals and assists to be had … It was still a game to me. You went out to win every game. It wasn't like you dreaded it … It's not like we went out there and never touched the puck. We were getting our chances."

Like Degenstein, Jim Ursaki came to the team partway into the season—as Bob Miner replaced Wayne Jacques as coach—again emerging from Junior B in hopes of bolstering the Foxes. "I always enjoyed playing because it was a higher level of competition," he said. Goaltender Terry Brennan said hockey was hockey in his world. "We were friends on the team. The guys that came out still wanted to play hockey. We did it all because we just liked the game," he said. Still, Marshall Hamilton—who played as a 17-year-old over the latter part of the season—said there were times it was hard to find players who wanted to wear a Silver Fox jersey. "The hockey on the ice wasn't necessarily the toughest part. We'd show up at the bus for a road trip and there might have only been 12 guys, and we'd be phoning around to see if we could find two more guys who wanted to play," he admitted. "It might be a case where we were playing North Battleford one night and Prince Albert the next, so we'd tell them to pack a suitcase because it was an overnighter." That being said, Hamilton—who would go on following the season to play four years with Yale University in the United States and then on to a five-year Canadian Football League career—said it was "a good learning experience when I was quite young."

At the time, the mounting losses were almost a mystery to the players and Silver Fox staff. Degenstein recalled Duane Fagerheim, a coach at the time, repeatedly telling the team, "'It's so simple, you guys.'" Fagerheim, who now resides in Saskatoon, was the team's third coach of the year, following Jim Miner and Wayne Jacques into the hot seat. "Basically it was either take over and give them a hand, or let them fold the tent," he said.

But even the simple sometimes evaded the Silver Foxes. Ursaki recalled a Monday game when they were to host Prince Albert, who had played road games in Weyburn and Moose Jaw Friday and Saturday. "I remember the coach saying Prince Albert could be had because they had played two games in three nights," he said. "They beat us 21–3. It was just unbelievable." In another game to end the season, a Notre Dame player was on the hunt for seven points to win the scoring title, said Ursaki. "He ended up getting eight or nine." The Silver Foxes sputtered through to the end of the season.

But a nucleus of 200 or 300 fans still came out to watch. "I don't know if they came out to see how badly we'd get beat, but it was the same faces in the stands," joked Ursaki. Hamilton said in some ways the Foxes became fan favourites in Regina, where the Pat Blues also played as part of the SJHL. "We were a bit of an enigma," said Hamilton. "The Pat Blues had a good team and we sort of had the leftovers (he himself was cut from the Pat Blues in training camp). But the Pat Blues were getting maybe 10 fans out and we were getting a couple of hundred. Everybody knew we would eventually win a game and they wanted to be there." Degenstein said the team always believed they could win if the bounces went right for a change. "We were a pretty upbeat group," he said. "It wasn't a constant downer or anything. You just went out and had your shift and tried to do your best because it was sport … We were young men and knew how to make the best of it. We weren't hanging our heads or anything." Ursaki agreed the mood stayed positive. "The guys on the team worked hard and we had a good time, too," he said. "You might think we'd feel really ashamed and not want to go out and play, but we went out there every game. In a lot of cases we thought we could win the game. But we just didn't."

Hamilton said it was sort of frustrating, inasmuch as the Silver Foxes could be solid one night and terrible the next. He recalled back-to-back games in Melville, the first game an 18–2 loss, and the next night keeping it to a 3–2 deficit. "The team was bad, but the players weren't," he said, adding that when everyone was on, the Silver Foxes could play some good hockey. Fagerheim said the core players were dedicated. "It was a bunch of kids who wanted to play hockey and they did their best," he said. Admittedly, playing on an SJHL team in a city where the Western Hockey League Regina Pats were the main attraction helped deflect scrutiny over the losing streak. "Nobody really knew us," said Degenstein. "We weren't the big shots in town. It was a little easier to maintain an up attitude, because we weren't in a city where we were the thing. We were pretty low profile."

When they were hassled by those outside the game, Degenstein said it was a case of remembering "we were good enough to play in the league and the guys doing the joking weren't." Unfortunately, practice time was often at 6 a.m. or even nonexistent for the team, and the players agree that hurt how they performed in game situations, no doubt extending the losing streak. "I can remember going to practice at the Al Ritchie (rink) at 6 a.m. on a school day and there would be only four or five players out there," said Hamilton. Bad practice times, coupled with less than 100 percent commitment from players and management, proved a bad mix for the team, he added. So somehow the Silver Foxes always found a way to lose, to the point the streak made stories in the *Globe and Mail* and other newspapers all the way to the United States, said Degenstein.

Through it all, some players made life for the others bearable.

Degenstein said Ursaki, for one kept, the mood in the dressing room light. "He was a solid player, but more importantly he had one of the best senses of humour," Degenstein said. "He was just fun to hang around with." That helped, agreed Hamilton, who related an incident in Swift Current. "They were crushing us and there was a fight, which was one thing we usually won," he said. "Jim Ursaki wasn't a fighter, he was the comedian, but he goes over to get in as the third man. He just bumps into the guys fighting and the referee yells 'You're outta here!'" recalled Hamilton. "Jim says, 'Thank you!' and skates off, waving to the fans."

Degenstein said ultimately the top players on the Silver Foxes were as good as any in the league. He pointed to Hamilton, who would go on to Yale University, and to teammate Brent Lewis, who would later in his SJHL career win championships as a member of the powerful Prince Albert Raiders. Goaltenders Terry Brennan and Doug Koffler were also steady in spite of the losses. "These guys were first-class goalies. They by themselves could keep it close," said Degenstein. "But there were nights they were facing 75 shots. I think the worst I saw was 121 shots in one game against Prince Albert," said Brennan, a game that ended up something like 18–1 for the powerhouse Raiders. "Fifty or 60 shots were not uncommon," he added. Brennan said players were always fighting for personal points. "Other teams just never let up. Players came in thinking they could get some easy points. If guys wanted points they knew they were easy to get when they came to play us. They just kept coming every shift, but that kept us going, too." Degenstein still said the Foxes had faith in their goaltenders. "If our goalies were hot, we could be competitive with anybody," he said. "We just didn't have enough talent all the way through the team." "I think we had highly skilled guys among our top six or seven players," said Ursaki. "After that it was pretty slim pickings."

Still, it would be the 17-year-old Hamilton who would stand out. Although he joined the Silver Foxes well into the season, after competing in a high school football season in which he won the provincial title with the O'Neil Titans, he would emerge to wear the team captain's C, as well as lead them in scoring, and be named their Most Valuable Player of the season.

Surprisingly, other teams were never excited about playing the Silver Foxes, said Degenstein. "They hated to play us, because they were always expected to win," he said. When the losing streak finally ended, it did so with a true sense of drama. It was against the Moose Jaw Canucks, in a game that would be knotted 5–5 after regulation time. And finally, in overtime, the yoke of losing was cast off on a goal by Brent Lewis only 53 seconds into the extra frame. The goal ended a streak stretching back until January 28, 1974, and the previous SJHL season. It was also the team's 45th game of the year. "Moose Jaw was really upset they lost," said Ursaki. As it was, Hamilton recalled the Silver Foxes had a 5–1 lead with eight minutes left in the game, and watched as the Canucks clawed back to tie it.

But as memories tend to do, Hamilton's memory was not quite in sync with the story told in the Regina *Leader-Post* of the day. They recorded the February 3, 1975, meeting just a little differently. The Silver Foxes did jump out to the lead as Rick Edwards scored twice and Degenstein added one, for a 3–0 lead after 20 minutes. Seconds into the second period, Mark Pillar made it 4–0. Then the Canucks took over, scoring four unanswered goals to tie the score before the second period came to a close. Thirty-seven seconds into the third, Degenstein gave the Foxes another one-goal lead, but the Canucks would tie it at the 16:31 mark to force overtime, creating the opportunity for Lewis to break the streak and provide the Silver Foxes with their only win of the season. In reading from the *Leader-Post* story, Fagerheim related that at the time he was quoted as saying after the game that he was "happier than hell for the guys. They're the ones that did the work." Fagerheim said he felt they would win the game, and even when they allowed the lead to slip away, he told the players between periods to stay focussed and they could win the game. Brennan, who was dressed but was on the bench watching teammate Brent Dark guard the Fox net against the Canucks, said the win was possibly less exciting than many might think. "I don't know if it was a relief … We obviously didn't want to keep the streak going. That's why we kept competing," he said.

But memories of the win fade. "I do remember the big party at the Italian Club. At least it started up there," said Brennan with a laugh. Hamilton, who was on the ice having earned an assist on the winning goal, said it was strange that the chain of losses made the team, at least temporarily, famous. "I remember being at the Italian Club and Harvey Kirk, the CTV anchor, coming on the television. It was the opening line of the newscast and fireworks were going off in the background, and he was saying, 'the Silver Foxes have finally done it,'" said Hamilton. Fagerheim related that CKCK television, having heard of the Silver Foxes' 3–0 lead after the first period, even sent a camera to the game. "They were so excited by the prospect of a win, they forgot to put film in the camera, so there's no record of it on film," he said. At the team's awards banquet, the puck that ended the streak was raffled, with Hamilton the winner. It is a memento still stored safely in a trunk.

Now, years after the fact, it's not the losing streak or the Lewis goal that comes quickly to mind when the players remember the Silver Foxes. "I guess more than anything it was the friendships, the friends a guy meets along the way," said Brennan. "You would go into another rink and their fans were really getting into it and it motivated you, too. It was quite a rush." And in the end, tying on a pair of skates and hitting the ice to play Canada's favourite sport was still an act of love for most players—even the Silver Foxes in a season where wins were a rarity. "You have good years and you have bad years and you can learn from both," offered Hamilton. "The message is just do your best every day. If you do your best, the score doesn't matter, because you can walk away with your head high.

"And it's just a game. It's not life," he concluded.

Hat Trick Welcomed to "The Show"

Going from being a contender in the National Hockey League to joining a team in decline was a tough move for Gregg Sheppard. But a knee injury that ended his career prematurely was harder still to accept.

Sheppard was born in The Battlefords and was one of the last players to advance to the NHL through the old system of signing players, rather than them being drafted. He was the property of the Boston Bruins. Sheppard started his professional career in the minors in the 1968–69 season with Oklahoma City in the now defunct Central Hockey League. It would be the 1972–73 season before he got his chance with the Bruins, scoring 24 goals and 50 points in his rookie year. A season earlier, he had earned the CHL's Most Valuable Player Award on the basis of 41 goals and 93 points.

Sheppard said the Bruins almost waited too long to make the call for him. "Really, after my third year (in Oklahoma City), I was thinking if I wasn't picked up by one of the expansion teams I might not go back." When Boston called, they wanted Sheppard to initially head to the Boston Braves, their farm team in the American Hockey League. He wasn't interested in making what he saw as a sideways move, away from a city he knew. "I seriously thought about quitting hockey." But he made the trip east and played only eight games with the Braves before becoming a full-time Bruin.

Sheppard's NHL dreams, though, had begun back in The Battlefords, taking up the sport when he was seven or eight. "I got introduced to it by my cousin, who was already skating." That was at the old Battlefords Municipal Rink, now a furniture store, in the community Sheppard returned to when his hockey days were over, at least on a competitive level. Sheppard said playing hockey as a kid in his town meant lots of ice time. "It was a town of about 1,500 people at that time, so everybody seemed to play every sport." Hockey was an instant hit with the young skater. "As soon as I started playing I loved it." At the time, Sheppard said he was a huge Toronto Maple Leafs fan, with defenceman Dick Duff being his idol. "He was such a key player. He was sort of their unsung hero. When I was playing hockey outside underneath the street lights, I was always Dick Duff."

About the time Sheppard reached his first year as a teen, he recognized that he was better than most players on the ice his age. That only fuelled his desires. "My hopes and dreams were to play in the NHL." As a midget, Sheppard's team made it to the provincial finals, only to lose to a team from Moosomin in a two-game total-goals series. At 17, Sheppard had an opportunity to get some on-ice schooling in the sport. He joined the Beaver Bruins, a juvenile team playing in the "Big Four" senior league. The team was funded by Boston. While he said the young team had greater speed than some of the adult players they faced, the experience and tricks of the game had to be learned on the fly by the kids to compete. "Some of the fundamentals of hockey were really pounded into you," he said, both during games by opponents and by coaches after.

Sheppard moved next to Estevan, a team in transition, playing in three different leagues in the three seasons he spent with the Bruins, who were at that time still supported by Boston as well. Here again Sheppard went to a final, this time a national one against Niagara Falls, Ontario. Playing the initial games on neutral ice in Montreal, the Bruins fared well, but when it moved back to Niagara Falls, Estevan faltered. "By that time the writing was on the wall," said Sheppard, noting they lost the series in five games.

The losses in championships as a midget and with Estevan would be washed away in his time with the Boston Bruins, where Sheppard's career had something of a fairy-tale start. The first game for the player who was a Maple Leaf fan was in Toronto at the fabled Maple Leaf Gardens. Sheppard admitted there was a certain amount of awe at the morning skate at the hockey shrine in Toronto; he even ventured into the stands just to sit in one of the fans' seats to get a feel for it. When practice ended, he took a pilgrimage through the Gardens. "I walked through the halls of Maple Leaf Gardens and saw all the pictures of players I had dreamed of as a kid up there. It was everything I ever dreamed it to be and it was more than that, too."

The fairy tale continued into Sheppard's first game at Boston Gardens as well, where he scored a hat trick in front of the Bruin faithful in an 8–6 win. "The adrenaline was flowing that night," he admitted, adding that after working to get to the Bruins he wanted to prove he belonged there. He would go on to score 24 goals in his first season as a Bruin. Hat tricks seemed to be a trademark in certain game situations. With family making the trek to Edmonton to watch Sheppard for the first time, he did it again, scoring three in an 8–7 loss.

For the next six seasons, Sheppard would be a solid performer on a team filled with superstars—Phil Esposito, Gerry Cheevers, and John Bucyk among them. He would score 155 goals as a Bruin, lined up initially with Dave Forbes and Terry O'Reilly, and then with Bobby Schmautz and Don Marcotte. Among the 155 goals would be a long-standing record with the Bruins, the fastest two short-handed goals, at 21 seconds, coming against the then-Atlanta Flames. He would score seven short-handed goals one season to set a record at the time as well.

The best player Sheppard played with, in his mind at least, was Bobby Orr, a defenceman he often teamed with, playing the point on the power play. "It was pretty easy to play on the power play with Orr," he said with a laugh. Sheppard said he always used to tap Orr's pads before a Bruin game, and tell him he had to "work hard to overcome" his inefficiencies as a player. The two remain friends who still chat on the phone.

The highlight, of course, came in the spring of 1972, when Sheppard would once more be in the hunt for a title, this time a chance to sip from the Stanley Cup, captured by the Bruins. The thrill of the Cup lasted six years, before Sheppard was traded to the Pittsburgh Penguins in 1978 and another less fulfilling chapter in his hockey career was launched. "I've always explained it was like going from the major leagues to the minor leagues," he said. At the time, hockey in Pittsburgh was far down the totem pole of sports, with the football Steelers being recent Super Bowl winners and the baseball Pirates playing well, said Sheppard. That meant a different attitude permeated the Penguins. "It didn't have the mentality in the dressing room that we had to win every night," said Sheppard. "In Boston there was always the feeling we had to win every game."

In his first year with Pittsburgh, the Pens did well, actually occupying first for a chunk of the season, until perennial power-house Montreal turned it up a notch, Sheppard said. However, after the first year, there was a virtual sell-off of players, as the Pens faced financial woes. Each trade seemed to weaken the team further. Although the game was more of a chore in a city where hockey was anonymous and dedication to winning wasn't a priority, Sheppard wanted more than the four seasons he played there, thinking two or three more seasons, or until he was 35, was reasonable. Then a collision with teammate Randy Carlyle in practice changed everything for Sheppard and his hockey career. Sheppard's knee was injured. Rest was prescribed, but once he was back on the ice, a hit by Ron Greschner aggravated the injury. "The knee ballooned right up," said Sheppard. An operation followed, and then a second, but to no avail. "I was done."

The realization his dream career was over was difficult to deal with. "It was really hard. My expectation was to say no when I wanted to say no," he said. "I just wanted the opportunity to say I've had enough and walk away on my own terms." Making it more difficult to accept were the words of a Saskatoon specialist, once he was back home, who questioned the operations done to the knee, suggesting arthroscopic surgery could have repaired the knee sufficiently to continue playing.

Suddenly Sheppard was looking at a life beyond hockey in an era when a 10-year career in the NHL didn't mean a fat bank account. "I could have stayed in Pittsburgh or moved back to Boston. I had job opportunities in both," he said. Instead, he closed the circle, returning to The Battlefords to partner with an old friend in a realty business. Sheppard would coach a little, following his son Brent to AAA Midget. A promising young player with his eyes on an American college scholarship, Brent would suffer a career-ending injury to his shoulder in junior hockey.

While there have been hardships, Sheppard has no regrets. "I owe everything to hockey. I thought about playing in the NHL, but I wouldn't have dreamed that I would play 10 years."

Sheppard did eventually return to the ice, but on a friendly level back home in The Battlefords, on an old-timers team. "I work up enough sweat to drink some beer," he said with a chuckle.

Longevity Marks Storied Career

Johnny Bower should be the poster boy for perseverance in hockey. Bower, a National Hockey League star whose career spanned some 13 seasons, put together a career that culminated with his induction into the Hockey Hall of Fame. It's a story that, while telling the tale of exceptional play, doesn't sound particularly different from a number of other hockey greats. The story of how he got to the NHL makes Bower's story more compelling. He spent more than a decade in the American Hockey League (AHL) before finding a permanent spot on an NHL roster. In fact, Bower was 28 before he played his first NHL game with the New York Rangers, in a one-season visit to the "show," before once again heading down to the minors. He would be 34 before finally getting a chance to stick with the Toronto Maple Leafs. Along the way, Bower would set a record for wins by a goaltender in the AHL—a record that remains intact.

Many might have hung up the pads, especially after his rookie season with the Rangers—going 29-31-10 with a 2.60 goals-against average and playing every minute of the Ranger season—wasn't enough to keep him in the big league. The thought of quitting never occurred to him. "What really kept me playing was the childhood dream of wanting to be like Frank Brimsek, 'Mr. Zero,'" said Bower, who was a huge fan of the Boston net-minder. "That was the goal that led me to just keep going. I never thought of quitting hockey. I just loved hockey so much." Bower said being replaced by goaltender Lorne "Gump" Worsley in New York after one season did shake his confidence, but not the dream. "I just about lost my confidence there," he said, adding that New York was a tough place to play. "It hurts a lot inside when they let you have it, if you let in a bad goal."

Fortunately, back in the then-familiar AHL with Providence the following season, Bower overcame the jeers and doubts. In fact, his play earned him the Les Cunningham Award as the AHL Most Valuable Player in 1956, 1957, and 1958. Of course, AHL awards were not something new for Bower, who also captured the Harry "Hap" Holmes Memorial Award for fewest goals against in the AHL in 1952, 1957, and 1958. He was also first-team all-star in the NHL five times, and won three AHL league championship Calder Cups with Cleveland.

Finally, Bower would get his big break, becoming the proper-ty of the Toronto Maple Leafs. It was a change in organization the goaltender initially balked at. "I didn't really want to come here," said Bower, who stills lives in Mississauga, Ontario, not far from the Maple Leafs home. At 33, Bower told Toronto executives, "I don't think I can help the Leafs." He was by then comfortable with the AHL Cleveland Barons. "I wanted to know where I'd be if I didn't make the team? What would happen if I didn't report?" Told he would be suspended if he failed to attend the Toronto camp, Bower did secure assurances that if he was sent down, it would be back to Cleveland. Although the Leafs would have a dozen goaltending hopefuls in camp that fall, Bower didn't have to worry about a clause stating where he would play if sent back down. He made the team, and stayed a Leaf. "My dream came true. It had never died," he said.

Bower said it was "just great" playing his first game in the NHL with New York, although the team was a last-place club, but it was equally sweet re-emerging with Toronto half a dozen years later. He said finally making it was in large part due to a dedication to hard work. "I kept on working and working. I always believed in hard work. I believed what you did in practice was what you did in a game," he said. The work paid off, too, as Bower would be an integral part of Leaf success for a number of years to come, including winning four Stanley Cups.

He points to the first and last Stanley Cups as the highlights of his playing days. "The first Stanley Cup (in 1962), what a thrill that was," he said. "I held the Stanley Cup—I didn't want to part with it. It was the greatest feeling in the world." Bower also looks back on his last Cup with the Leafs in 1967 as special. "The 1967 Cup was a great feeling, too. They said we had too many old guys on the team to win. We had about nine guys who were over the hump," he said. While the Leafs might have had some older players, the experience of the likes of Red Kelly, Carl Brewer, Tim Horton, Bower himself, and goaltending mate Terry Sawchuk propelled the team to the championship. "The Chicago Blackhawks had a real powerhouse that year," said Bower, but the Leafs upset the Hawks in seven in the semi-finals, then beat Montreal in the final for the Cup.

Bower said he had a good feeling about the Leafs the minute they acquired Sawchuk. "I told them then we were going to win the Stanley Cup," he said. The two also shared the Vezina Trophy as the NHL's top netminder in 1965, the first time the award was ever shared by teammates. Bower had won it on his own in 1961. Sawchuk was a quiet man, with his own troubles at the time, but Bower said he helped make the Leafs better. "I learned a lot from him just by watching him." Bower said it was important to always keep learning. For example, he found himself fighting the puck and realized, watching Sawchuk, "I was coming out to cover the angles too fast and my stick was off the ice." Sawchuk wasn't the first goaltender Bower picked up pointers from. Although he would become noted for his ability to poke-check the puck away from opposing players coming in on net, it was not a technique he developed. It was something he picked up from netminder Chuck Rayner. "He'd come out on the ice with me and have me dive at pucks after practice. It drove me crazy, but that goalie stick can be real handy," he said. "I have to thank Chuck Rayner for the help he gave me."

Even with pointers along the way, Bower said there were some exceptional shooters to face in his day. He put Maurice "The Rocket" Richard at the top of that list. "He drove me up the wall. I could go to church and light candles and he'd still score a hat trick," he said. Gordie Howe also drew comment. "I kept him in the league for a while," said Bower with a chuckle.

Not a bad career for a kid from near Prince Albert who grew up poor. He was the only boy in a family of nine children. The family never had much money, so proper hockey equipment just didn't exist for Bower. He made his goalie pads, used horse manure "road apples" as pucks, and his father cut crooked tree branches to shave into sticks. Initially, even hockey wasn't something Bower's father said he should pursue. "My dad wasn't too wild about hockey. He told me once, 'It's too rough for you to play. You'll get hurt. You should play soccer.'" Although Bower also enjoyed kicking a soccer ball around, he and his father soon came to realize that he loved hockey best, a game he started out in as a goaltender. "I never played forward in my life, well, maybe in a street game," he said. When it became apparent hockey was his game, Bower's father built a backyard rink. "That's where I learned my hockey, playing against kids from all over the neighbourhood."

Like many kids in Saskatchewan in love with the game, Bower hung around the local rink—the Prince Albert Minto Arena. It was there he met Don Deacon, a senior player who bestowed on Bower his first skates, size 12s, so big for his young teenage feet he had to stuff the toes with paper. "But I managed to use them," he said. Bower's hockey would get something of an interruption with the outbreak of the Second World War. He lied about his age, then 15, to enlist, going with a dozen other young men from the P.A. area. When they found out his age, Bower was held back in Canada, while the others were sent overseas. "The majority of them didn't come back," he said. He would eventually go over, but never did see action.

Upon his discharge, Bower returned home after four years of service, still young enough to play his final year of junior. After junior it would be Cleveland Scout Hub Wilson from Saskatoon who convinced Bower to head to the Barons and the start of his 25-year career, which culminated with his retirement in 1970 at the age of 46. Bower stayed active in hockey after retiring, first as a goaltending coach and then as a scout for the Leafs. Then in 1976, there was one more memorable moment for the ageless netminder, an induction into the Hockey Hall of Fame. The induction was well-earned. In 534 regular-season NHL games, he had 37 shutouts and a goals-against average of 2.53. He had five shutouts and an average of 2.58 goals-against in 72 playoff games. "What a great honour that was. I never dreamed I'd be inducted into the Hockey Hall of Fame," he said. "I was just so thrilled. I just couldn't believe it. I was in the Twilight Zone for about two weeks there." And the induction ceremony itself was one of high emotion, said Bower. "I was more nervous than facing Gordie Howe or Bobby Hull on a penalty shot."

Little Guy, Big Heart

There's an old adage about it not being the size of the dog in a fight, but the size of the fight in a dog. Dennis Polonich might be the poster boy for that old saying. Certainly, Polonich never caught a lot of attention on the ice because of his stature. The Foam Lake-born player stood only 5-foot-6, and it took a dripping wet jersey to tip the scales at 165. To Polo's credit, he always had that sweaty jersey, though, through hard work with a gritty edge.

Polonich's hockey started as it does for so many prairie boys, on outdoor ice. "We lived on a farm and obviously made our own rinks, cleaning off sloughs and the dugout." When Polonich started playing on organized teams in Foam Lake, it was thanks to his grandmother. "I had a grandma, bless her heart. Her name was Katie. I would move in with her. I basically lived with her throughout the winter. It was too hard to drive back and forth for practice and games. We didn't have a lot of money and only had one vehicle. If I didn't play I'd catch the school bus and go home. If I played I'd stay." Polonich said his grandma lived only a few blocks from the town's hockey rink, a building that had a draw on him from the outset. "I would see the lights on if the rink manager was there. If he was there, I was gone. I was basically a rink rat and helped him all winter."

There was also lots of ice time for a young player with some solid skills. Polonich spent one winter playing on three separate teams: his own bantam-aged team, the school team, and the Foam Lake Flyers senior team in the Fishing Lakes Hockey League. He won back-to-back championships with the Flyers in a league where he learned a lot playing with and against grown men, many twice his age. "I was playing with men. Sure, there were many times I just had to tough it out," he said. "It certainly helped me become a competitive player." But he learned as well, tipping his hat to three people in particular: Steve Sidlick, the local rink manager, and players Harold Sandberg and Keith Harkness. "Those three individuals kind of looked after any young guys who played for the senior team. They took us under their wings."

As a midget, Polonich headed to Moose Jaw to play, ending up on the same team as Clark Gillies. "I wanted to move away and play a better brand of hockey," he said. He again stayed with family to keep costs in line. The move away from home was a huge step. "I remember my mom crying, but that's what I wanted to do. I had no money and didn't know how I was going to survive, but I wanted to do it." Polonich tried out with the Saskatoon Blades, but failed to make the team, so went home. Back in Foam Lake, it was the word-of-mouth aid of Herman Hordel that gave Polonich his first big break, a tryout with the fabled Flin Flon Bombers of the Western Hockey League. "He was a goaltender who played in Flin Flon. He told Patty Ginnell about me," he said. Ginnell was the coach of the Bombers and he invited Polonich north. "Because I had gone through the experience of Moose Jaw and Saskatoon, there was no way I was going to Flin Flon and not going to make it," he said. "So I got on the bus and went. I remember the bus turning down Main Street and there was a big fight on the street in front of a bar. I remember wondering what I had gotten into. But you grow up fast. You learn to survive."

Even before the bus ride, though, Polonich had to deal with the issue of skates. "I had a pair of old Black Panther Bobby Hull Specials ordered out of the Sears catalogue ... I wish I still had them," he said. He dreamed, like most young players, of owning a pair of CCM Tachs. He had heard if he made the Bombers, he'd get a pair. "I phoned Patty Ginnell from my grandma's place, we didn't have a phone, and asked Mr. Ginnell what kind of skates I should bring," he said. He was fishing for a promise of the Tachs. "He said, 'Bring the fastest ones you've got, kid.'" Polonich, of course, made the Bombers and got the Tachs. "It was quite a thrill going to the local hardware store and getting fitted for the new CCM skates," he said.

Making the Bombers, though, meant impressing Ginnell. During an early scrimmage, Polonich figured a good way to do that was to block a shot. "I had never blocked a shot. No one had ever taught me how," he said. So down he went, blocking the shot just below his ribcage and above the stomach. It knocked the air out of him, but he wouldn't stay down, getting up and skating off the ice in definite pain. "I looked over at Ginnell and he sort of winked at me and said, 'That a boy.' I knew then I was making some progress."

It was Ginnell's influence that Polonich credited with making him the player he turned out to be. "He moulded me into that tenacious little guy who was tough to play against," he said, adding that life with the Bombers was rough and tumble. "Teams went up there on weekends. We played them awful tough on the Saturday to make sure we softened them up for Sunday." It was so tough in Flin Flon, the story used to go around of teams having a second car following the bus collecting gear, "because guys were throwing it out the window so they could say they couldn't play because they'd forgotten some of their equipment at home."

Polonich played gritty enough that when Ginnell attended the National Hockey League draft in the spring of 1973, he was able to convince Detroit to take a flyer on the tough little forward. Polonich said his junior coach basically told the Red Wings, "He's a tough little guy. You won't regret drafting him. You've just got to give him a chance." In the eighth round, 118th overall, the Wings gave Polonich the chance he had dreamed about. While growing up a fan of the Toronto Maple Leafs, and in particular Dave Keon, come draft day Polonich wasn't fussy. "I didn't care where I went," he said. "That Detroit took me was just unbelievable … It's a storied franchise. It's an Original Six team." After the draft, the Wings flew their young picks to Winnipeg, presenting them with contracts to sign. "I just signed it. (He still has the pen in a frame in his basement.) I didn't have an agent or anything." The deal contained a $7,500 signing bonus and $24,000 a year. "And I didn't care. I was going to Detroit to training camp."

After his first year as a pro, Polonich did end up investing $8,000 in a cabin at Fishing Lake near his home town, which he still owns, a far cry from the million-dollar mansions some rookies can afford today. Although the money wasn't huge and he was an eighth-round pick, Polonich remembered with pride that his career outlasted each Red Wing pick taken ahead of him that year. Of course, that meant nothing in his first training camp. He was a centre on a team with the likes of Alex Delvecchio, Red Berenson, and Marcel Dionne, already at the position. Polonich realized the minors were his likely assignment. "Back then young guys didn't make the teams in their first year. Back then you persevered in the minors two or three years."

When he did get his first call-up, he remembers his minor

league coach Doug Barclay scratching some helpful hints on a piece of hotel stationary for Polonich, a piece of paper he still has. The little hints included old hockey axioms such as keep your head up, let the puck do the work, and pay attention to defence. The call-up was a huge event for the young forward. "Just stepping on the ice with Delvecchio and all the guys was great," said Polonich. "I knew how hard I had worked to achieve that dream." Polonich does recall one night during camp in his second season, when he was a last-minute fill-in for Marcel Dionne, who was feeling ill. He took to the ice wearing Dionne's sweater, unbeknownst to most people in the stands. "Lo and behold we have a brawl. I leave the bench," said Polonich. The feisty young Wing knocked out a St. Louis player to chants of "Marcel, Marcel." They thought Dionne had become a tough guy over the summer.

After two years in the minors, Polonich made the jump to the Wings, spending the next five complete seasons in Detroit. It was an auspicious start for Polo, scoring his first two NHL goals in the same game against Colorado. His first fight, which was more his style than goals, was also successful, taking on Brad Park. "I did pretty good in that one," he said with a laugh.

Over his career there were numerous tougher fights, including a trio of other Saskatchewan players with an edge: Clark Gillies, Dave "Hammer" Schultz, and Dave "Tiger" Williams. In his 390 regular-season games, Polonich would score only 59 goals and 141 points, but added 1,242 penalty minutes. The style made Polonich a fan favourite, with 15,000 fans at the old Detroit Olympia often starting chants of "Polo, Polo." "As my career progressed, I was sort of cast in that checking role. I played against all the other teams' top lines," he said.

Of course, Polonich might best be remembered for an incident he barely remembers. He goes into the corner with Kansas City's Wilf Paiement on Oct. 25, 1978. Later, Paiement would allege Polonich's stick came up on him as Polo played a backhand. Whatever the motivation, Paiement baseball swung his stick, hitting Polonich across the face. "He two-handed me with a baseball swing. He just shattered my nose, not just broke it. It was crushed like an eggshell," recalled Polonich, who was knocked out cold. Paiement received a 15-game suspension from the NHL, but the real news was when Polonich sued him in civil court, winning a settlement of more than $1 million. A case of its kind was unheard of at the time.

"I had thought about the consequences many times," he said. "You were going into territory nobody had ever gone. Nobody had ever done that in hockey ... There were times some people were jealous and looked at me a bit differently." Polonich said the case "didn't set off a chain reaction" of similar cases. He said for him it was something that made sense. "When you have opportunities, why wouldn't you explore them?"

Although the case is what many people remember when thinking of Polonich, he said his whole career was something he took pride in, including two Stanley Cup semi-finals, a Calder Cup victory in 1980 with Adirondack in the American Hockey League, and a Turner Cup in the International Hockey League with Muskegon in 1986. Still, no Stanley Cup hurts. "That's one of the regrets that I had," he said. "I just wish we'd had more stability in Detroit." Over eight years there was a change in ownership, about 10 coaching changes, and a handful of general managers.

Another regret was several seasons of bouncing between Detroit and the minors as his career came to an end. "I blame it a bit on naïveté. I was brought up to work hard, to be loyal, and to be honest," he said, although he felt "a debt of gratitude" to Detroit for the opportunity they provided, "and, guess what? I got the carpet pulled out from under me." It was a disappointment, but one he has used since, as he now acts as a player agent.

Between playing and becoming an agent, Polonich was a coach for 12 years, winning a Royal Bank Cup national championship with the Yorkton Terriers. After hockey, it was a natural. "I had to start all over again and I just kept coming back to hockey," he said, saying he liked coaching. "I was good at it. I still have a knack to read people, to get in their heads and see what makes people tick." Now, as an agent, Polonich said he tries to roll his days as a kid in Foam Lake, his NHL experience, and the coaching into a package that can help young players. And, of course, he credits the game for everything. "I owe it all to hockey and I'm forever grateful. I don't for one second take it for granted."

Fulfilling Childhood Dreams

Jeff Odgers grew up on a farm near Spy Hill with two dreams, one to be a hockey player and the other to raise cattle. In Odgers' case, hockey would enable him to fulfill both dreams. "I started playing hockey when I was four years old," he said. "I grew up like every kid who lived in Saskatchewan, wanting to be a hockey player. As far as I can remember all I wanted to be was be a hockey player." Odgers said he recalls as early as kindergarten being asked what he wanted to be when he grew up. The answer came naturally: "a hockey player and a farmer."

The connection to the farm was obvious, since he grew up on one with his family. His family also played a role in developing Odgers' passion for hockey. Two uncles, Mark and Greg Faul, played for the local senior team, the Spy Hill Hilltops, and the young boy with hockey dreams saw himself playing the game as his uncles did. Born in 1969, Odgers was able to play hockey in the small community of Spy Hill, only two and a half miles from the cattle ranch operated by his parents. "When I was a kid we had a team in every age group," he said. When he returned to the area to start his own cattle operation just over three decades later, the rink still stood, but the community no longer had minor hockey, testament to the declining population of rural areas. Still, there was never any doubt in Odgers' mind he would one day end up back in the area, on a farm, raising cattle.

But there was a long road from his days in the hometown rink and the start of his own cattle operation. It was a road he began to seriously tread as a teenager when he moved to Saskatoon to play AAA Midget hockey with the Blazers. While a step up in hockey calibre, the move to Saskatoon was toughest simply because of the move. "Moving away from home was the harder adjustment than to the hockey," said Odgers. He had attended Grade 10 in Langenburg, near his home, with 60 students. In Saskatoon, he attended Evan Hardy with 1,200 students. "That was a pretty big adjustment itself."

The stay in Saskatoon was a short one. After one season, Odgers, at 17, headed to the Brandon Wheat Kings of the Western Hockey League. "I went to their spring camp after the Blazers season was over," he said. He felt he performed well. "I thought there might be a chance for me to stay. I went there the next fall and made the team." What was ahead as a Wheat King was four years of education, with limited on-ice results, at least when it came to team success. "We made the playoffs my third year and we won one game," he said. Being on a struggling team did become frustrating as the seasons passed in Brandon. "I think the first couple of years you're just happy to be there, to do whatever you can to stay there," he said. However, as he matured in the league, Odgers admitted he was concerned by the Wheat Kings' lack of success in the standings. "Winning teams were being scouted more than the bottom teams," he said. It wasn't that the players weren't trying, but success always seemed a goal or two out of reach. "We were close to making that jump, but we just couldn't get over the hump."

For Odgers, his National Hockey League draft year came and went without him being selected. However, thanks to Chuck Grillo, who was holding a developmental tryout camp, Odgers had a chance to show scouts they had missed something in not drafting him. His play at the camp earned him an invite as an unsigned player to the camp of the Minnesota North Stars. Brandon coach Doug Sauter knew it would be a big step for Odgers, considering he had not been drafted and did not have a contract. He told Odgers at the time he would have to make a statement on the ice as a player so they would be writing his name down on the charts during camp. "I fought six times in my first two games," said Odgers with a laugh, noting the rough stuff had always been a part of his game. In his first game, Odgers proved a willing participant, taking on noted NHL tough guy Basil McRae in four fights in the first scrimmage. "Pierre Pagé came down out of the stands and told them to get us off of the ice, he'd seen enough," said Odgers with a laugh. "They were pretty good scraps." At the time, as an unproven rookie, it was simply Odgers challenging someone he recognized as a force in the NHL. As years passed, he said the tables were turned, with him often challenged by young players looking to get noticed in training camp. "I've been in that situation myself," he said, adding that in the case of McRae, "he understood what I was doing."

The camp didn't lead to a spot on the Stars' roster, but with San Jose on the verge of a new franchise, it did net Odgers interest from the fledgling Sharks. "That was pretty rewarding," he said. "I knew I'd made it, that I'd get a place to play hockey, and that's always what I'd wanted, and what I'd worked for." However, the Sharks were still a year away from hitting the ice, so Odgers was put on a personal services contract and sent to Kansas City in the International Hockey League. "It was a great year. Kansas City was a great city," he said. He liked the mix of young guys trying to climb the hockey ladder and experienced players there to stabilize the team. "It was one of the most fun years I've had." But the next season the Sharks did hit the ice and Odgers made the step into the NHL with the team. "Definitely there were more opportunities with an expansion team to make it," he said, "Obviously the depth of an organization isn't great when it's starting out."

Of course, in the first season the Sharks took it on the chin most nights, but losing wasn't something that wore on Odgers that year. "Everything was new. Every arena we went to was new. I was playing against guys I had watched play when I was a kid," he said. "Every experience that season was new. It kept you refreshed." Odgers recalled just how in awe a young player can be breaking into the NHL. The Sharks were playing the Los Angeles Kings. Odgers skated out for a faceoff and realized he was on the same ice surface as Wayne Gretzky, Dave Taylor, Jari Kurri, Larry Robinson, and Paul Coffey, all future Hall of Famers. "It was amazing. It was kind of like, 'You're here playing against these guys in the same league. Wow!'" he said.

Odgers also found he liked playing in the sunny climate of California, suggesting it was not a problem getting up for hockey, even in the balmy temperatures. "It was great," he said. "There were so many things to do to get your mind away from hockey and the rink." He said if the focus is always on hockey it can wear on you over a long season, to the point it's detrimental to one's play. By getting away, it refreshes the mind, although once you walk into the rink and lace up the skates, you know hockey is your job.

For five seasons, Odgers would be a Shark, seeing progress quickly, moving from expansion franchise in year one to the playoffs in his third season. In their first taste of post-season action, the Sharks upset Detroit, taking Game Seven of their series, then lost to Toronto, but again forcing the Maple Leafs to Game Seven. "That was a great experience," said Odgers, who added that success was not a regular thing for him, having to go back to minor hockey to find a team he played for with a better than .500 record. Odgers would then become something of an NHL gypsy, being traded to Boston for one season, then on to Colorado for three. It was with the Avalanche that Odgers came closest to the Holy Grail of the Stanley Cup, losing to Dallas in the semi-finals. "I was one series away from going to the Stanley Cup finals," he said. The next season Odgers was moved to Atlanta, as the Avalanche went on to win the Stanley Cup. "I went to Game Seven when they won it against New Jersey. I was happy for the guys I'd played with, but I was really wishing I could have been skating around with the Cup, too ... It's the one thing I wish I could have experienced. Every time I see that team at the end carrying around the Cup there are a lot of emotions."

As an Atlanta Thrasher, Odgers was once again on an expansion team, not as a youngster looking to build a career, but instead as a sage veteran there to help players develop. It was a role he said he was at ease with. "It was a young team kind of looking for some experience. I always enjoyed the room and being with the guys," he said. "I enjoyed seeing the young guys come up and seeing them become established in the league." Still, after his third year, Odgers knew it was time to hang up the skates, even before the call came from the Thrashers that they would not be re-signing him. He walked away from the game after 821 games in the NHL, with 75 goals, 70 assists, and 145 points, plus a robust 2,364 penalty minutes.

With the NHL behind him, it was time for a trip back to Spy Hill to pursue his other boyhood dream of running a cattle ranch. "I really wanted to be on the farm," he said. He knew if he had tried to hang on, it would have only delayed the inevitable, and taken him away from his young family (he had married a girl from Kansas City). "In family ways I was missing out on a lot of stuff."

For Odgers, though, hockey is still a big part of his life. He coaches both his sons in minor hockey, enjoying it all except when he sees a youngster displaying a lack of effort, something he knows you have to put forward to be successful. The game is still important for Odgers as well, as he packs the gear and heads out to small rinks to play senior hockey with the nearby Rocanville Flyers in the Triangle Hockey League. "Just because I retired didn't mean I had lost the passion for the game," he said. "I need hockey. I need more than rec hockey." So Odgers takes the bumps and bruises of senior hockey, keeping his long-held dream alive, and enjoys every minute of it. "I'm getting a lot more ice time, too. I'm even getting on the power play sometimes. That's different for me."

Even in Silence He Felt the Pride

Michael Merriman may not hear like everyone else, but he hasn't let that slow him down—even on the ice. Merriman, who was born at Springside and played minor hockey in Yorkton, has become one of Canada's leading deaf hockey players, becoming a leader for four straight Canadian National Deaf teams.

Team Captain Merriman has enjoyed three tours of duty with the national team at the world stage. The first experience with the National Deaf team came in 1995 at the Winter Deaflympics held in Finland, a year in which Canada returned with a silver medal, losing to the United States in the gold-medal final. Four years later in Davos, Switzerland, Merriman and the national team would return from the championships with the gold medal, the first in the history of the Canadian team. Merriman said he has a difficult time figuring out what the first gold medal meant to him. "Personally, I'm not sure what it means, and I probably won't until I'm older," he said. "It's kind of an inside good feeling ... but I'm elated for the program ... It's great for Canada."

The success has earned the Canadian team and deaf program its own display in the Hockey Hall of Fame, which Merriman said is a major step. "I donated my gold medal to them," he said, adding that the decision to give up his medal "was a simple one. It was an honour. That's the way I looked at it … It's great. Guys who go to the Hall of Fame who are hearing impaired now have something to aspire to."

In February 2003, the Canadian team headed to the Winter Deaflympics in Sundvil, Sweden, where Team Canada successfully defended their gold medals, with Merriman leading the way. "This is something I cherish as we defeated the Americans 5–2 in a deciding match for the gold medal and went 5–0 during round robin play. We had more depth and a solid group of younger players who were ready to accept the responsibilities to be a champion. Things are looking very good for our program for the upcoming Olympics," said Merriman.

On a personal level, Merriman was also pleased with his play at the 2003 championships. "I played a solid game throughout the tournament. As one of the older players, I really wanted to show up and compete hard on every shift to show the young guys it can be done. I led the team in scoring for the third Olympics and lost the tournament leading goal scorer for the first time by a point to a Russian player," he said. It was the way Merriman wanted to play, given he felt retirement might be beckoning. "It was a special time at this Olympics because it might be my last one as a player," he said. "With our young core of players waiting in the wing, it might be time to pass on the torch. I have already joined the organization on developing summer programs and forming player contacts for the future of our program. I have been working very closely with the general manager, Roy Hysen. I have made a commitment to this program for life and whether I play again or coach at the next Olympics is to be determined. This is a very special program that has made and will continue to affect people in a very positive way."

While Canada and the United States were favourites heading into the Games, Merriman said other countries are becoming more of a factor. "Finland is really getting strong. They helped us in '99 in the round robin when they upset the United States," he said. "And Sweden is not far behind." Russia (due to a lack of funding), Switzerland, and newcomer Germany are still developing programs, added Merriman. Preparing for the 2003 Winter Deaflympics, Merriman said the Canadian program took on a more serious attitude. The Canadian Championships were held in March in Winnipeg and 25 of the top players were listed for the team.

Being captain of the Canadian team for three Deaflympics is just another step in a long list of successes for Merriman. For three seasons he taught at Notre Dame College in Wilcox, Saskatchewan, while coaching the school's Argos team in the Saskatchewan AAA Midget Hockey League. For Merriman, Notre Dame is clearly part of his hockey background, having played two seasons for the Saskatchewan Junior Hockey League Hounds before accepting a scholarship at Ohio State University.

It was as a Hound that Merriman's character was clearly seen. "It was during my second year of junior hockey at Notre Dame. Things had gone well personally, considering I already had my hockey scholarship with Ohio State University locked in for the next hockey season. But things were not going well as a team—in our third year in league play we were not going to make the play-offs for the first time," he recalled. "We were a young team and had a ton of injuries which never allowed us to form a solid run with the whole gang during league play. For an example, I was out at one time for six weeks with a dislocated elbow just when I was near the top three in the SJHL scoring at the time. The doctor predicted that I would miss the whole season, let alone come back in six weeks. A lot of our injuries were very serious.

"So from the previous season losing to Nipawin in the league final, to not making playoffs was very hard to take as a player and as a team. It was the first time we were struggling in the SJHL. As veterans, we wanted to finish our commitment to the team, Notre Dame, and the Bear (Coach Mackenzie). We had a young team and thought it was important to set an example to them for the following season. It was very tempting when the Bear informed us, myself, and Dave Karpa that Yorkton was interested in us coming over to finish the season with them ... I remember being excited and very interested to take the offer ... Yorkton was home, and Dennis Polonich had an influential effect on my hockey career from attending his hockey schools back in the day. There were a million reasons to jump at the opportunity, but after a few talks with my teammates, and soul searching from within, I decided to turn down the opportunity from a mindset of how I wanted to be remembered at Notre Dame when I left. I did not want to be known as a quitter. Just because things were not going well, doesn't mean you should be jumping ship.

"I guess loyalty was very important to me in those days. I wanted to finish what I started, something my father and mother had instilled in me as a person. I would be lying if I don't think once in a while what it would have been to finish the year with Yorkton. As a kid I used to think I would play for the orange and black someday, and then hit the NHL. But neither of those happened. I do not regret my decision to this day because it was not a decision based on material gain, or what-can-you-do-for-me attitude, but simply for being committed to myself in finishing what I started. And the loyalty to (those) whom I gave my word to."

From the ups and downs experienced at Notre Dame, it was off to Ohio State University and a solid college career as a

Buckeye. "The first two years at Ohio State were very good. I had a better first year than the second. The first year I was in the top five in scoring on the team and played a lot," said Merriman. "The second year was a bit of a struggle, sophomore slump maybe, but things did not go as smooth as the first year. Over the two years of playing I won a player of the month a few times, athlete-academic awards, and lettered in both seasons." But then, mirroring the downturn in his final season at Notre Dame, things were less successful the final two years at OSU. "The final two years were very difficult to take as a player and as a person," said Merriman. "For certain reasons, myself and the coach started not to see eye to eye on things. My playing time diminished to healthy scratches and eventually to not playing at all. This was all about ego and personality conflicts, but this is all water under the bridge now.

"What matters here is that everyone comes to a time of their life in hockey when things either move forward or you come to a halt. Regardless of the reasons of the halt, one has to learn what life is after hockey. Again, I had a few offers to play elsewhere during my last two years at Ohio State, but again I still chose to finish what I started. It was the first time in my career where things were not progressing as expected. I think everyone develops a bit of a sour taste when hockey comes to a halt, and feel they lost their identity as a person. I felt those feelings, but because I chose to continue my commitment to Ohio State, I was able to overcome those feelings. As a result, I learned that during my whole career in hockey I was the person I am, not because of hockey, but who I choose to be through the experiences I had. This was a valuable lesson, as I got the best of both worlds, played NCAA hockey, finished my college degree, and learned a lesson so valuable that it gave me a solid ground to stand on after college."

The level of play at the Deaflympics which followed was not quite up to the junior and college hockey of Merriman's past, but competing comes with its own rewards, including representing his country and aiding deaf athletes by becoming an example of what can be accomplished. "There's a significant difference in skill and level of play," he said. The top two lines on the team are likely to have players with major junior and college experience, but the third- and fourth-line players tend to be from Junior B, or those who played AAA Midget and are now playing senior hockey. "But it doesn't matter what level of hockey you're playing, the same things have to come into line to win a championship," he said.

Merriman counts bantam coach Barry Marianchuk among those who most influenced his hockey. He said his parents, coaches in Springside minor hockey, the Davies family (Carman, Clark, Dean), and Kelly Lovering are among those who have most influenced his hockey. And like any kid, he had his favourite players he aspired to emulate. "Players I looked up to as a kid were Guy Lafleur, Lanny Macdonald, Darryl Sittler, and Tiger Williams," he said. "As I got older, the '80s Oilers hockey team, Mark Messier, Adam Foote, and Steve Yzerman, and in the management side of the game, I have always loved Glen Sather."

Merriman explained that in order to play on the National Deaf Team a player must have a hearing loss of 55 decibels (dB) or greater. In his case, he has 58/57 hearing loss. "I just sort of skimmed through," he said, which makes him somewhat unique on the team. Most players are considered totally deaf, and only a few speak orally. "When I first came aboard only two of us could speak orally in '95," he said. That has been one advantage Merriman said the United States has enjoyed. Drawing from its large populace, most players on their national team "are on the upper edge of the limit and they're able to communicate that much quicker." Communication is the biggest difference between mainstream and deaf hockey. "The challenges are different, communicating first of all," said Merriman. "But you work just as hard whether it's a hearing team or a non-hearing team."

Merriman said when he was first approached to join the national team he sort of balked at the idea. "I've been mainstreamed all of my life," he said. "In 1995, I had no idea what I was getting myself into. I thought there were players more deserving than me." It was a case, in part, of coming to terms with his own hearing loss. "I tend not to want to look at myself as hearing impaired," he said. "I look at myself just like anybody else. It was never difficult fitting into the mainstream side of things. I was captain or assistant captain many times for the teams I played for. It was difficult with the deaf at first because I was a minority for the first time in the dressing room with the deaf team. If anything, the characteristic of being hard of hearing gave me a chance to become a leader with the mainstream teams: It isolated me differently at first but once I showed the group my skills, determination, and heart, I was able to lead my peers."

Then a friend helped him realize the honour involved in being on the national team. "Once I got over that hump, I now look at it as a lifetime commitment," he said. While saying his playing days may be over with the 2003 team, Merriman said he could see himself involved as the team's general manager or in a similar capacity into the future. Merriman has already expanded his involvement in deaf hockey beyond the playing surface. "We're building a national hockey school program for the deaf," he said. The plan is to have national team practices that will coincide with camps for players as young as eight, who will learn from the national team members. "We'll get them to love the game and eventually fill the shoes of the old bucks like me," said Merriman.

When asked about the greatest hurdle a young deaf player has to overcome, Merriman said, "This is a tough question for me to answer as I never lived this experience, but I have come to learn isolation, the gift to interact spontaneously in a normal conversation. From a dressing room setting to the last-minute instructions before a faceoff are hurdles," he said. "Just imagine playing the game without the seventh player (the crowd) motivating yourself. They overcome this through positive attitudes, commitment to better themselves, and staying focussed."

So will creating the youth program be more difficult than playing at a high level? Merriman simply sees it as a new challenge in the sport he loves. "The challenge is different, but I look at it as no different from being a player," he said. "I love the game, love interacting with people, and from this challenge I can give back to the game what it helped me do. As every program is insignificant unless a leader or person steps up and makes it a significant program, I view it as my role to make it a significant one."

Six-Decade Drought Ends

A 60-year hockey drought came to an end for Saskatchewan in April 2001, thanks to the Lloydminster Border Kings. The Border Kings captured the Allan Cup Senior AAA Hockey Championship with a 7–2 win over the Petrolia Squires. The win marked the first time a Saskatchewan team had won the 93-year-old trophy since the Regina Rangers earned the cup in 1941.

Goaltender Jason Clague earned MVP honours at the four-team Allan Cup tournament. He said the victory was made sweeter by the Border Kings having hosted the Allan Cup Tournament in 2000, but losing in the final on home ice. "We had a pretty good run ...when we hosted the Allan Cup," said Clague. "We ended up getting beat in the final."

Clague came to the Border Kings with a history of playing well. He started the 1994–95 hockey season in the Western Hockey League, but he would end up making history with the Saskatchewan Junior Hockey League's Yorkton Terriers. Clague joined the Terriers shortly after the season's start, when the team's record was at 1–7–1, and upon his arrival he would help carry the team to within one point of top place in the league's South Division. By the time his season with the Terriers was over, Clague's effort could only have been termed great. He posted a 32–21–2 record, faced 2,297 shots, and racked up 3,210 minutes, both tops among SJHL goaltenders. So it was no surprise when the Terriers named Clague their Most Valuable Player.

However, Clague would take it a step further, becoming the first netminder in league history to be named the MVP of the season. It was also the first time a Yorkton Terrier had earned the prestigious award. "I wanted to do everything I could to help our team win," said Clague.

Clague admitted that, in retrospect, his Terrier season was one he was happy he had an opportunity to play. "Lee Odelein was coach and he treated me really well," he said. "He was a really good guy to play for." It helped, too, that Clague was coming home, since he had grown up in the Stockholm area. "It was close to home, so family and friends were there to watch me," he said.

Merv Mann was captain of the Border Kings and a six-year veteran of the team. He said knowing of the long-time drought was part of the team's motivation. "We knew it had been years. We used that. Every little edge was important," he said.

Mann noted the loss on home ice in Lloydminster in 2000 was hard to take. "So many guys had stayed around and played that year," he said, adding that the players felt the team was solid and, after the loss, they feared they might never get another chance. The second time the Border Kings would not be denied.

Clague said the team was successful because of the commitment of the players. "The key for our team was the commitment our guys put into coming out to practice and to getting ready for games," he said. "None of our guys get paid. There are no superstars or ex-pros. It's just guys who love to play and to play together."

While the team came together over the course of the year, at training camp things looked somewhat bleak. "We had only six guys returning," said Mann, "and 10 new guys. We thought we had no chance, but then everything fell into place."

One of the moves was the return of Bill Thon as head coach, after two seasons away from the Border Kings. "When I first got back we didn't have much left, but it seemed every time we turned around somebody would come in that added to our team," he said. The team came together around a nucleus of four long-time veterans—Mann, his brother Morgan, Ray Neilsen, and Tyler Scott.

One of the arrivals was former SJHL player Trevor Rapchalk, who said that winning at the senior level means more than just playing hockey. "You've got to practise and play, but you've got to go to work at the same time," he explained. The commitment all the players made to the game made success just a little more special. For Rapchalk, being part of the Border Kings was a case of being in the right place at the right time. The season before, he was playing in the Yellowhead Hockey League, which folded. "It's kind of funny. I went to watch a Yorkton-Melville game and Jason Clague's dad was there watching his younger brother (Michael) play for the Millionaires," recalled Rapchalk. Talk turned to hockey and the Border Kings' loss in the 2000 final. "He (Clague's father) said they could have used me last year when they hosted it, and said I should go this year because they were making another run at it." Four days later Rapchalk was in Lloydminster as a Border King.

Clague said the quality of play at the Allan Cup ranks with the best hockey he has played, which suggests it's a solid product, given that Clague has played with the Red Deer Rebels in the Western Hockey League and Yorkton in the Saskatchewan Junior Hockey League, and has spent two years with the University of Regina Cougars in the CIAU. "It might not be as fast as the

WHL, because they're younger guys," said Clague. "I think it would be comparable to university hockey." He added, "Almost every guy you're playing against has at least some junior hockey experience."

Rapchalk, too, has had his taste of hockey, including not only time with the Yorkton Terriers, but a Royal Bank Cup championship with South Surrey in 1998. Still, he ranked the Allan Cup up there in his experiences on the ice. "It's right up there, if not on par with the Royal Bank Cup," he said. "You're dealing with older guys and some who are ex pro players…It's a little more heads-up."

Even with Clague's stellar hockey record, the Allan Cup win ranks among his biggest thrills. "It's the first championship I'd won since minor hockey," he said. "It's something I'm proud of and something the team is proud of. The year I had in Yorkton was a special one and I have a lot of memories from that, but this is a national championship."

Being on the first Saskatchewan team to win the Cup in 60 years only added to the significance of it. "Senior hockey in Canada is second to none," said Clague, adding, "I think Saskatchewan is on par, or better, than any province in Canada."

Mann said it might actually be getting tougher to reach the top level in senior hockey. "I think it's getting harder every year. There are more ex-pros playing. Quebec has become a money league now. I think the big thing is staying healthy. You play five games in five nights at the tournament. We're not used to that grind." That is a factor that makes simply getting to the Allan Cup tournament difficult, although in their winning year the Border Kings swept Paradise Hill and Battleford in Saskatchewan, and Grunthal, Manitoba, on the way to the finals tourney.

Clague said that having the 2001 tournament on the road might actually have helped the Border Kings. "I definitely think it was easier playing on the road, especially in that final game," he said. In front of the hometown fans in 2000 the Kings were a little "tight." "When you're on the road, you're loose."

Loose the Kings stayed, winning their opening game of the round robin after falling behind 3–0 to Dundas, Ontario, in the first period before bouncing back to tie it in the same frame. "They were Ontario champions," said Thon, adding that the win was viewed as critical. "In a tournament like that, playing round robin, it's so critical winning that first game and taking some of the pressure off."

Game two was against Stony Plain, Alberta, a team Thon said were long-time rivals of the Border Kings. "It was the best game we ever had against them." Lloydminister hit double digits that night, winning 11–3. Next up was the host team Petrolia, eking out a tie, the closest the Kings came to a loss throughout the playoff run. Meeting in the final 48 hours later, after Petrolia ousted Dundas, the Border Kings asserted their dominance. "We felt pretty good about the final game," said Thon. "We had our chance in the round robin game. We thought we could win."

Mann also felt the game was theirs, especially after it started. "Basically, five minutes in we knew it was our game. They had their chances to get back into it, but I thought throughout we felt we were in control." With the 7–3 win the Border Kings avenged their home ice loss, and ended the province's long drought. Defenceman Mann and Clague would be among five team members named tournament all-stars, along with forwards Ian Monroe, Scott Hood, and Greg Brown.

As an added reward for the big win, the Border Kings would represent Canada in Poland in the fall of 2001. They met the Polish national team in a three-game set, tying once 3–3, losing a close one 7–6, and dropping the final game 5–0. "They were a little disappointed they didn't beat us by more," said Mann, adding Poland had just moved up to the "A" group at the World

Championships and were looking to the series as a tune-up. "They had some good players, but some who weren't quite as good."

Clague said facing Poland, winners of the "B" Pool World Championships that year, was amazing. "That was an unbelievable experience. They were a really good team—really skilled. To visit another country and experience some of their culture—it's something the guys will remember the rest of their lives."

The Border Kings hope to repeat their championship win, and are scheduled to host the Allan Cup Tournament again in 2005.

Cultural Component to Team

The Beardy's Blackhawks are unique among teams in the Saskatchewan AAA Midget Hockey League, in that they are owned by, and play on, the Beardy's Reserve near Duck Lake. The team originated out of the St. Michael's Residential School program, joining the league in 1995 when the residential school closed. The building actually burned down in 1998. At the time, two local reserves took over operations of the team, Beardy's and One Arrow, with the team playing as the Willow Cree Thunder. However, as Beardy's took over sole control of the franchise, the Blackhawks were born.

Mel Parenteau has been with the team since 1998, and he looks on the First Nations-based team as an ideal situation for players drawn from all across the province, including Aboriginal communities often overlooked by hockey recruiters. "What I like is the cross-cultural aspect of this team," he said, pointing to the 2003–04 edition of the team as an example of what he means. The team has seven players who are status Indians, five who are Métis, and the rest Caucasian. "They're all working together, sweating together, and becoming better together. It's an awesome thing to see. You can't put a money value on it." As far as the young hockey players are concerned, they're all simply teammates, regardless of the ethnic makeup. "Kids don't care what colour you are as long as they're having fun and playing hockey."

The team was a good fit locally in the sense that Beardy's had a brand new sports complex built in 1995, allowing the team to play on Reserve rather than in nearby Duck Lake. "It was a good opportunity for youth development through hockey," said Parenteau. However, running a AAA Midget team is not easy for a small reserve. "It's not easy, it's a costly venture. It takes about $200,000 a year to run the program," he said. The local band pays both Parenteau and coach Dale Grayston's salary, and then hands over fundraising to their long-time general manager to cover the remaining costs through programs and donations. "I find different ways to make that happen," he said. "There are a lot of different ways of finding the money to run the program ... While it's been tough at times, we've been successful."

The success did not come initially. In fact, in the team's second season, then head coach Wes George was let go after a 0–12 start to the season. Grayston, who had been an associate coach, was asked to take over. He said it wasn't a case where George was at fault. "A lot of times the coach is the one let go, but you have to be realistic about the talent level, too. It was our program's fault that we faltered to a two-win season ... We knew we were in tough," said Grayston, who added that his philosophy was simple, to take some positive steps to stabilize the program. But he would pilot the team to only two wins in 44 games. "It was very difficult. It was difficult on the players, too." The situation was such that the team let some players go and others walked away, so that by January they had only 13 players on the roster, two of those netminders. "It's difficult to try and come up with Ws when you have six or seven fewer players," said Grayston.

The future of the team came into some question, and it wasn't until August that Grayston was asked to return as coach. "Again, you're behind the eight-ball because most of your recruiting is done in the spring. We kind of went into camp that year with no set idea who our players would be." In fact, the talent level was such that Grayston said camp became more of a hockey school, teaching skills. However, through patience, the Blackhawks attracted some late cuts from other teams, and climbed to ninth spot, one out of the playoffs.

Being based on reserve, the Blackhawks face an interesting challenge, as players are living in a number of communities to attend various school classes, then driving to Beardy's for three-days-a-week practices and league games. Players live in Saskatoon, Martensville, Prince Albert, and other communities, as well as in nearby Duck Lake and on the reserve. Parenteau said it makes for some interesting logistics, especially for players commuting almost an hour each way. "It's a big, big commitment for these kids, but that's just the way it's got to be," he said.

Of course, the onus is still on the Blackhawks to build a contending team. When it comes to Aboriginal players, Parenteau said, "We pretty well know what's out there." It helps, too, that the team is coming to be seen as a natural place for young native players to advance to. "When they're ready, they phone and register for our program."

While Parenteau's long involvement with the Blackhawks has added stability, coach Grayston has been with the franchise since its St. Michael's days. That long involvement is an asset, said Parenteau, because players like to play for a coach with such a reputation and experience. The combination of coaching experience and ties to Aboriginal communities as a pipeline for talent came together for the 2000–01 season, when the Blackhawks won the Saskatchewan title, the Western Regionals, and advanced to the Air Canada Cup Tournament held in Prince George, BC. "That was a good team we had when we lost out at the Air Canada Cup," said Parenteau. "That was awesome." The Beardy's Blackhawks finished the regular season that year with a record of 26 wins, 13 losses, and five ties for 57 points, which placed the team in second place out of the 12 teams in the league. The team finished the last month of the regular season with nine wins against only one loss, setting the trend for the playoffs ahead. They went through the Saskatchewan playoffs with a record of nine wins and only two losses. The next step was the Western Regionals in Moose Jaw where they went a perfect 4–0, earning their trip to B.C.

The success of the Blackhawks that season, such a short time after their 2–42 campaign, didn't come as a major surprise to Grayston, who was named league coach of the year for 1999–2000. "I think the only way you can get through things like that is to have confidence what you're doing with the program is making a difference in these young men's lives," he said. "It was just a confidence factor. We were treating the kids right and they responded." Grayston only considers the winning year slightly more memorable than any other. "I've got to be honest with you. Even the two-win season was a good year for me. The 13 guys we ended up with are still guys who phone me," he said, adding that wins are not everything. "We've had 150 guys come through our program. Some years we win. Some years we don't. It doesn't mean the season wasn't rewarding just because we didn't win the championship." Grayston realizes that hockey is not the biggest thing kids learn on a team such as the Blackhawks. "It's the lessons you're going to pick up from being around good people, which is more important than learning how to pass the puck."

The success of a championship after only six seasons was a pleasant surprise, although there were signs the team was jelling into a contender. The Blackhawks were the 2000 Ice Mania Tournament Champions in Prince Albert, Saskatchewan, and finished fourth at the internationally recognized Mac's Tournament in Calgary. Parenteau said any successful team gets there by hard work "and finding the right chemistry." Leading the Blackhawks was goaltender Jonathan Krahn, who was the Saskatchewan Midget AAA Hockey League (SMAAAHL) Goaltender of the Year and 2nd Team All-Star, as well as the Air Canada Cup Western Regional Most Valuable Player. "You have to have that guy in the playoffs if you're going to be successful," said Grayston.

The Blackhawks have been fortunate in having a number of stand-out netminders. For example, B.J. Sklapsky, who would go on to win the Royal Bank Cup with Humboldt of the Saskatchewan Junior Hockey League, was the top Sask AAA Midget goaltender for 1999–2000. Chance Gieni, who would move on to the Notre Dame Hounds of the SJHL, would go one better as a Blackhawk, being named league MVP for 2001–02.

While stellar goaltending has become something of a team tradition, so, too, is finding quality native players. Such was the case in the team's championship year. Part of the right chemistry came from local players Brent and Riley Gardipy. Brent earned the Air Canada Cup Western Regional Top Defenceman Award. Having players from Beardy's First Nation on such a successful team was important, said Parenteau. "That was a bonus, too. It helps the program, but there is still lots of work to be done in our own backyard to develop young players coming up for the future. We've got lots of work to do to make it the way we would like to see." Grayston said local talent is a key for any AAA Midget team. "Obviously we're really proud of what we've been able to accomplish, but it wasn't easy. We've been blessed by being able to convince a lot of really good area players to come here." As an example, he pointed to Richie Regher, who was a bantam draft selection of the Western Hockey League Kelowna Rockets. The Rosthern-born player was a Blackhawk at age 15, before heading to the WHL. "I think from that moment on we became a hockey team," said Grayston.

As for Aboriginal players, Grayston said for Beardy's to be successful, they have to attract those players. "The key for our program is we have to identify the high-end native players, and get them here, and hope they'll buy into what we're doing." For example, Rick Peeteetuce suffered through the two-win season, but came back the following season and made the top 10 in league scoring. Grayston said that type of development is gratifying. Parenteau said he looks forward to the future with Beardy's, but adds he knows there are still strides to take, especially among Aboriginal communities and their hockey programs. "The future looks good for us," he said. "There are some good kids out there, but lots of development is still needed."

Grayston said that while some native players have the same skill levels, many suffer by coming from smaller communities where access to weight training, nutritional counselling, and other important facets of hockey development simply don't exist. He said kids need to appreciate that they have to mould their bodies these days. "The body is the vehicle to take you someplace in hockey," he said.

Of course, a lot of satisfaction comes from watching Blackhawk players progress in their hockey careers after graduating from the midget division. "You can see a lot of the kids making strides, not only as hockey players, but as good young men down the road," said Parenteau. In 2004, there were seven Blackhawk graduates playing in the Western Hockey League and 18 in the Saskatchewan Junior Hockey League. "We're quite happy when

we look at their stats on the computer and see how they're doing. We like to keep track of them." Parenteau himself is a former
SJHL player with the 1970–72 Prince Albert Raiders. And having Beardy's certainly has opened doors for First Nations players.
For the 2003–04 season, there were 10 Aboriginal players in the
entire league—seven of those with the Blackhawks. "Without this
program there wouldn't be many of them playing," said Parenteau.
"The program is really needed by First Nations."

Grayston said as the future unfolds he hopes the Blackhawks
evolve. "I hope that down the road we will be able to be an all-
Aboriginal team," he said. He'd love to see a former native player
come back one day to coach the team. "Hopefully, one of them will
want to come back and work with young people, and take over the
team." Whatever the future holds, the Blackhawks will strive to
continue their traditions, building in a league Parenteau looks at
as the premier league of its kind. "We're in a very, very good league
here. The Saskatchewan AAA Midget League is probably the best
in Canada, I might even say in North America." From Parenteau's
point of view, he wants to stay involved with the Beardy's program
because of what it means to the Aboriginal community. "I'm just
proud to be part of this program," he said.

Net Results Were
Usually Positive

When you start looking for the elite in goaltending, the name Glenn Hall usually enters the conversation early. A Calder Trophy winner as the National Hockey League's top rookie following the 1955–56 season, Hall burst onto the NHL scene in a major way. As a rookie he played in 70 games, recorded the first 12 shutouts among the 85 he would eventually amass, and had a sparkling 2.11 goals-against average. The 12 shutouts left him one short of the league record at the time. Not a bad start for a kid from Humboldt, Saskatchewan.

"I played all my minor hockey there," he said of his hometown, including moving on to play with the Humboldt Indians of the Saskatchewan Junior Hockey League. By the time Hall was an Indian, he was a goaltender, but he actually started out playing forward. "I probably was in peewee when I started to play goal. I think that really helped me. So many goaltenders in the old days couldn't skate. That was a real advantage knowing how to skate." Hall said that as a kid he always wanted to be playing hockey;

it was a year-round passion. "In the summertime you were just dreaming about the ice."

Hall would move to the next level, heading to Windsor of the Ontario Hockey League at the request of the Detroit Red Wings, the team that owned his NHL rights, and with which he would break into the big leagues a few seasons later. The move was his first away from his hometown, but Hall said he took the relocation half a country away in stride. "It wasn't tough. It was enjoyable. You were doing something you loved to do. Anytime there was a puck on the ice, I was in my element." Hall's time in Ontario was important when it came to developing his game. "The Ontario Hockey League was at the top of junior leagues in Canada then," he said, noting Guelph and Barrie won the Memorial Cup the two seasons he played in the league.

While Hall tipped his hat to all the coaches he had growing up, Jimmy Skinner in Windsor was singled out. "I thought he was great. But I was lucky to have the type of coaching I did all the way along." That being said, Hall admitted goaltenders didn't get a lot of special attention from coaches, not like today when many teams have goaltending consultants to work with. Hall, himself, would fill the role of consultant for several seasons for the Calgary Flames. "It was trial and error," he said. Even as a consultant with the Flames, there was only so much he could do. "I told them it's a minefield out there, and I can tell you where to step to miss some of them."

When Hall began in the NHL, teams carried only one netminder to most games, meaning there wasn't even the opportunity to discuss things with a back-up who at least understood the position. "You didn't get much chance to talk about hockey." What Hall did hear was advice on a goaltending style he came to appreciate was simply wrong if he wanted to stop the puck. "They wanted you to stand up and not touch the puck if it wasn't going to hit the net." It was a style that Hall saw as too stiff to be effective as the game evolved to hard shots and more deflections of point shots. He felt that, as a goaltender, he needed greater mobility than a stand-up style allowed. He explained that with his pads tight together there was no freedom to side slide across the net to catch deflections. The result was a new style, one which became known as the butterfly. The style allowed Hall to splay his pads along the ice with his knees practically together. If the puck was heading for the top half of the net, he could push off his skates and pop back up to a standing position. "When I started with the butterfly, it created some problems," said Hall. "There was a lot of controversy, but it simply made sense." Hall's decision meant playing with his legs slightly apart, creating better mobility. "You can't move your legs if your pads are together. It was common sense the butterfly would come into it." Hall would be in the NHL before he fully adopted the new style.

Before the NHL, he played four years in the minors. "I learned in the minors, certainly," he said of his one season in Indianapolis and three with Edmonton of the old Western Hockey League. Hall had played a few games with Detroit before his big year as a rookie, which he said helped him ease into the NHL. "I'd been up with Detroit for a few games, so I had something of a taste for it," he said. Making the big team was still a huge thrill. "It was great. It was something you could never imagine." While he had learned at every level of the game, Hall said the NHL was an education as well. "It was great hockey. The great players always educated you on things. They had moves you didn't expect."

When it came to picking the toughest shooters he faced, Hall said one needed to look only as far as those who regularly topped the NHL in scoring. "They were the top scorers because they could do things other guys couldn't." Of course, one player stood out, first as a teammate and then as an opponent when Hall moved to Chicago, and that was Gordie Howe. "In my mind he's the greatest player who ever played. He was the total player. He was great offensively, very good defensively, and he was the toughest guy in the league."

Hall may have started his career in Detroit, but he became famous as a Blackhawk. Hall spent 10 seasons in Chicago and was placed on the all-star team eight times, five of those first team selections. In 1961, he backstopped Chicago to its first Stanley Cup since 1938. Hall would win the Vezina Trophy as the NHL's top goaltender in both 1962, playing 70 games, and in 1967 with Dennis Dejordy.

Strangely enough, after sharing the 1967 Vezina, Hall was left unprotected by the Hawks in the expansion draft that saw six new clubs join the NHL. Hall would be picked up by St. Louis, where he would play his last four seasons, helping the Blues add credibility to expansion. He said the team was better than anyone anticipated. "They (the established teams) didn't give anything to the expansion teams. It was just a bunch of old guys they thought were over the hill, and a bunch of young guys that they didn't think would even make it," said Hall. But St. Louis at least found a way to be respectable, starting in net with two veterans, Hall and Jacques Plante. The Blues would go to the Stanley Cup playoffs and, while losing four straight to Montreal, Hall would be named the Conn Smythe Trophy winner as the playoff's Most Valuable Player. The following year Hall would once again share a Vezina Trophy in St. Louis.

The success of goaltending on the Blues was a matter of coach Scotty Bowman's team philosophy, said Hall. "It was really complimentary to the goaltenders." It was a completely different mindset from his days in Chicago. "Chicago it was all run and gun. It was wide open just trying to out-score the opposition," said Hall. In St.

Louis, without gifted scorers, the whole team focussed on preventing goals. "Generally the best team wins the Vezina. We weren't the best team, not anywhere close to the best team," he said. "But it was a total team effort. The defence and the forwards were just as concerned about our goals against as the goaltenders were."

Still, not even Hall could stop every shot, and it would be as a Blue that one of the most famous goals of the game would get past him. The sight of Bobby Orr sailing through the air as his shot eluded Hall to win game four of their 1970 Stanley Cup finals series is a familiar image nearly 35 years later. It would give the Bruins their first cup in 29 years, and Orr would win the Conn Smythe Trophy. The goal is one Hall makes no apologies for, considering who scored it. "Bobby Orr, I have him just a little under Gordie Howe as the greatest player who ever played. He was an unbelievable hockey player. It wasn't like some slug scored that goal," he said, adding that the series was a mismatch from the start. "We had no business playing them in the playoffs. I imagine it was hard on them just going to overtime against a team like we had," said Hall.

While Hall had a long and successful career, only one Cup, with Chicago, would come his way, in 1961. "We were actually better after that. Unfortunately the opposition was better, too." Between them, Toronto and Montreal would win the next eight Stanley Cups in a row. "I'd like to have been on more, but it's hard to win." Even without more Stanley Cup rings, Hall saw the honours come his way after retirement. In 1975, Hall was inducted into the Hockey Hall of Fame; it was an occasion he viewed as "highly complimentary." However, an honour Hall looks at as just as fulfilling was yet to come. Hall is one of only five players to have their jerseys retired in Chicago—the others being Bobby Hull, Tony Esposito, Denis Savard, and Stan Mikita. Hall's number one jersey was lifted to the rafters in November 1988, the same night as fellow-goaltender Esposito's 35. "That's pretty good company," he said.

It's not surprising to see such an honour. Hall set a record for endurance that may never be matched. He played 503 consecutive games as a goaltender—all without wearing a face mask—although he would don one in the last couple of years of his career. The streak began on October 6, 1955, and continued until a game against the Boston Bruins on November 7, 1962, when he was forced to leave the game with a painful back injury. The endurance streak earned him the nickname "Mr. Goalie." As for playing without a mask, he admitted he caught more rubber with his face than he cares to remember. "You took more (stitches) than you wanted," he said. Even when Jacques Plante popularized the mask, a lot of people "thought he was a wimp." In his day, Hall said if you got knocked down you simply got back up.

An Eye for the Game

Hockey has been a lifelong passion and career for Dale Derkatch, although maybe not along the lines most hockey hopefuls dream about. Derkatch rose to prominence in hockey circles through three seasons with the Western Hockey League's Regina Pats. From the fall of 1981, through his three years with the franchise, he recorded 491 points, which remains a team record. The best season was 1982–83, when he scored 84 goals and added 95 assists for 179 points over 67 games. It would be a three-year span during which the Pats would enjoy at least 40 wins a season.

"When I look back I don't even remember playing," said Derkatch. "It's so long ago." The one moment Derkatch does remember as keenly as if it were yesterday is not one of joy, but of loss. It came in his final season with Regina when the team was playing Kamloops to advance to the Memorial Cup, "which is obviously what you are playing for as a junior." The Pats were up in the series 3–2 and were leading the sixth game by a similar score. With 20 seconds to go, Kamloops got a breakaway, which Pats goaltender Jamie Reeves thwarted. It set up a faceoff in the Regina end with only 12 seconds on the clock. The puck was dropped, a shot was taken by Dean Evason, and the red light flashed. The game was suddenly tied. The Pats would lose the game in overtime on a goal by eventual Winnipeg Jets first-round draft choice Ryan Stewart. The Junior Oilers would go on to take the deciding seventh game 4–2. "We were only 12 seconds from getting to the Memorial Cup," said Derkatch. "It's strange. I don't remember any of the goals I scored, but that's one thing I do remember."

Beyond the moment of regret, Derkatch talks in more general terms about his junior days. "I know I had good coaching and I had really good players to play with," he said. Two key linemates were Garry Leeman and Lyndon Byers, who were also teammates on the midget Notre Dame Hounds. The familiarity made the trio a potent force. "We didn't play much up until Christmas our first years and then it really took off from there," he said.

Derkatch remains humble about the points he accumulated as a Pat, suggesting his size played a role, in that he was nearly fully developed by that time. "I was the guy I was going to be. I wasn't changing a lot more," he said, adding that it gave him an edge in co-ordination and skill development. Derkatch's success may not have been just a matter of physical development, or a surprise, after enjoying two successful midget seasons with the Notre Dame Hounds at Wilcox. "We won the Air Canada Cup," he said, reflecting on the Hounds' 1979–80 campaign. The following season the team returned to the national finals, coming up short, but with Derkatch still taking home Most Valuable Player honours. Still, like his junior career, Derkatch said he hasn't retained a lot of individual memories.

Coming out of midget, Derkatch had not really thought of the WHL as an option to further his career. His eyes were set on joining the Prince Albert Raiders, then of the Saskatchewan

Junior Hockey League. As a Tier II junior player, Derkatch would still be eligible to receive an American college scholarship. The idea of education appealed to Derkatch and interest from WHL teams had been non-existent. Saskatoon had initially listed him, but never spoke to the flashy forward, and then traded those rights to Portland. Portland never spoke to him either, finally dropping his name from the list, where Regina picked it up. It was also paper shuffling, which Derkatch said he really wasn't concerned about. "My plan was to play Tier II in P.A. for a year, then go to North Dakota (for university)," he said. "My parents were big on me getting my education. So I had it all planned out."

Then, just on the eve of Derkatch packing to head to the Raiders, Bob Strumm with the Pats called, asking if he could visit and talk about Dale playing in Regina. Initially, Derkatch wondered why he'd bother taking up Strumm's time, but his father convinced him it was worth listening. The first thing Strumm did was take him to his hotel room, where on the bed lay a Pats Jersey with Derkatch's name and the number 16 he had worn as a Hound. The gesture by the Pats said something to Derkatch, who had long heard people say he was too small. It was a message often heard by the 5-foot-6 forward, who weighed 135 pounds at the time his junior career launched. "Everybody had always told me the next level would be too much," he said, adding that he had been convinced WHL people thought the same thing. "Obviously people there didn't think I could play because nobody talked to me, they dropped me from lists, they traded me." It was a different message from Strumm. He was telling Derkatch that if he attended the Pats camp, it was a 99.9 percent sure thing he'd make the team. "My dad asked me what I thought. I told him, 'He thinks I can play. I want to play.'"

But that still left the question of an education. In those days, the standard of offering WHL players some money for books and tuition after their playing days were over did not exist. "We wrote up an agreement. We did a deal with the Pats," said Derkatch. The deal would provide books and tuition to a Canadian college if he didn't sign a professional hockey contract within five years of graduating the Pats. He said he often wonders if his deal was a precursor of what was to come league-wide in the WHL. When his WHL career came to a conclusion, Derkatch was selected by the National Hockey League Edmonton Oilers in the draft. He was taken in the seventh round, 140th overall. Although most players clamour for a shot at the NHL, Derkatch chose a different path, again in part because of his size. Being a centre, it was a safe bet there was no room for him on the top two Oiler lines, thanks to the presence of Wayne Gretzky and Mark Messier. He was too small to be on the checking line, and few highly talented players languish on the third line. The contract offered was a three-way deal, with money decreasing if he was sent to either the American or International Hockey Leagues, and Derkatch said the money was not huge, coming well before the current explosion in contract dollars.

He began looking at options. "At that time, I got a couple of different offers to go over to Europe," he said, adding that he eventually packed his bags and headed to Italy after a call from Ron Chipperfield, who was coaching in Bolzano. "It was not very good hockey," he said. "But our team was pretty good. We won the championship." After two years in Italy, Derkatch moved across Europe to Ilves in Finland's elite league. There the hockey was of a much higher calibre, coming in an era before the best Finnish players were all in the NHL. "This was one of the best leagues in the world," he said.

Another league crown would come his way, as well as a new offer from the Oilers, but again the contract was a two-way deal, and he told the Oilers he wanted a contract for the Oilers or he'd go back to Europe. "They said, 'Then go back to Europe,'" said Derkatch. He did just that, playing for nine more seasons in Germany's top league. Again the hockey was not the highest calibre, but Derkatch said he realizes that more now than when he was playing. "I think the hockey, when you're playing, no matter what level you're at, you think it's pretty good," he said, adding that today he finds watching German hockey difficult because of its quality. In retrospect, he wishes he had at least given the Oilers and the NHL a shot at the time. "I wish now I had at least tried it," he said. "I had been playing a very high-end hockey. I had really been training at a high level. I should have tried it."

Following the end of the 1997–98 season in Germany, Derkatch hung up the skates, but he now spends more time than ever in hockey rinks. Today he scouts for the NHL's Washington Capitols, a position he was offered without really seeking it. "I said I'd give it a chance, but I knew nothing about it," he said, adding that the job "has got the feeling like hockey going one year to the next." Derkatch has been with the Capitols for six seasons now, up to 2004, and estimates he sees 160–180 games a season across Canada and into the United States, most at the major junior or college level. The position allows him to understand his own career better. "I can look back at myself and other guys and understand why they made it or why they didn't," he said, adding that he looks at his experiences in the game and sees his career as a successful one, even without making the NHL.

The Best of the West and All the Rest

It's a story of hockey development in a small town, similar to that of hundreds of young players, except in this case the player is a female. Brandy West grew up on a farm smack dab between two small Saskatchewan communities, making it a situation she still struggles with as far as picking a hometown. "My mom (Cindy) was really from Kennedy and my dad (Mike) from Langbank," she said. "We kind of did everything half and half. I went to elementary school in Langbank and high school in Kennedy. I played ball in Langbank and hockey in Kennedy."

It was in the Kennedy rink that West fell in love with a sport that, even in her youth, was still primarily the realm of boys. "I started hockey when I was seven," said West, who gravitated to the game because of a friend. "My best friend was playing hockey and she said I should come out and play."

That friend was Colleen Sostorics, who would become a long-time teammate for West before Sostorics advanced to the Canadian national women's team, capping her time there with the Olympic gold medal in 2002. West was thrilled to watch that game, an event that has spurred interest in women's hockey across the country. "Surveys have shown increased enrollments in young girls playing hockey," she said. But the gold-medal game was still years in the future when West made the jump to the game. "I loved to skate. I was in figure skating up until then," she said, adding that her family was at ease with her decision to change sports. "My family was pretty supportive of anything I did," she said.

There was no problem joining the boys, either. "In Kennedy and Langbank everybody had to play everything or you didn't have a team," said West. "If Colleen and I didn't play, the boys would probably have had to go somewhere else to make a team." West said there was no trouble fitting in, even with only two girls on the team. "When you're that age that didn't matter, and since we started out with them we were always just part of the team," she said. In some cases, West said she has heard of girls on boys' teams feeling somewhat isolated, having to dress in rooms away from the rest of the team, but that was never the case in Kennedy. "The coach just made certain rules and we all followed them," she said, adding that may have meant quick showers so the guys could take theirs, but that was about the only hardship.

West would continue to play in her home community through one year of over-age bantam hockey. Then it was time for a major commitment to continue the game. As a second-year midget (in Grade 12), she was on the road to join the Saltcoats Terriers, an all-girls team. "It was an hour-and-45 trip," said West. It was a trip made along with friend Sostorics and little sister Dana, who also played for the Terriers. With Bill Cudmore coaching, the Terriers played a season of games against mainly Regina competition, which West said wasn't what she had been used to, having played on a boys' club. "It wasn't quite as developed then. It was a slower pace. It's come a long way since I played at that level," she said.

There was also the adjustment to non-contact hockey, which meant a few penalties for the Kennedy trio. There is still a debate over contact. For West, the game as it is has its own unique merits. "I think it's a different game. Some people say they like to watch it more. It's more of a skill game. You can see plays developing. You can see the passes without a bunch of players crashing into each other," she said. With her Grade 12 complete, West was at a crossroads for her career as she contemplated college. She knew she wanted to keep playing and that the University of Saskatchewan had a women's team. But she wanted to attend the University of Regina. "I didn't really want to move too far away from home. I have a very close relationship with my family," she said. So West headed to the University of Regina, content with a decision to play hockey on a club team in the city.

"I was very frustrated in that, but still decided to do it," she said. But fate stepped in to help West's hockey development. A team was started at the University of Regina, and they joined the then-CIAU in her second season. Being in on the foundation of a new intercollegiate sport was "a pretty good experience, seeing the development of players who have come through the program, and how the program has improved," said West. She was a big part of that development. In 2001, she was awarded the Brodrick Trophy as the Most Valuable Player in Canadian college hockey on the women's side. She was the first Saskatchewan player to capture the major individual award.

Going into the season, expectations for the team were high. "The season before we just kind of got going and being competitive. We won some games," she said. "So we knew that year (2001) we had a pretty good team ... From the first game we played we knew we had a pretty good chance to make a run." The season did go well and then it was into the playoffs to face the power of the University of Alberta. "The U of A was sort of the 'Big Dog' team then, I guess," said West. "But we beat them in the playoffs." Taking the two-game total-goals series was a coming-of-age milestone for the Cougars and it put them into the national championship. While the team would not capture the title, it was a huge step for West and the team. "In previous years we kind of had one and a half lines that could really compete," she said. "That year we had three really solid lines and that's what it takes to compete."

For West, the season was capped with her personal award, an event she termed "pretty cool," but the specifics of her own season are not etched in her memory. They are kept in scrapbooks, she added. West said she had a good goal-points-per-game ratio, and she believes that accounted for a lot of her MVP award. "And most of my points were goals. That was kind of my job on the line," she said. West also credited linemates Julie Foster from North Battleford and Erin Tady of Regina with her own success. Tady's performance would earn her the CIAU Rookie of the Year honours. "We worked so well together. We scored a lot of line goals where we each figured in on it," said West.

West would play two additional years with the Cougars. Both seasons the university would host the National Championships, meaning an automatic berth for the University of Regina. Still, the championship would elude West and the Cougars. "We never quite got it. I'm very disappointed we didn't," she said, adding that it was hard to determine why. "There are a lot of factors that kind of go into it," she said. "Sometimes it's the bounces. Sometimes it's not reading the play right. It can be so many things … Definitely, I would have loved to come out of it with a title."

As West was starring on her own, friend Sostorics was making national strides. In 2000, West herself was invited to the under-22 national camp, one of 27 selected. After the first week of camp, five players were cut, including West. "You get prepared for a two-week camp and at the end of the first week you go into a room, and you're going home," she said. In retrospect, many have suggested West's MVP season was in part due to the cut, which fired her to excel. It's something she doesn't discount. Looking back, West also suggested CIAU players in the West maybe didn't get the chances at the national level. "In general, I think a lot of CIAU players didn't get a fair look, but now they're starting to go out to some of the games to see the players," she said. Now it's not unusual to see six or seven Saskatchewan players invited to the under-22 camp. West was the only one in 2000. That suggests the talent pool is getting deeper and that it's being recognized nationally.

With her university career complete, West said she wasn't ready to stop playing the game. In the summer of 2003, she was involved in efforts to establish a club team in Regina—named the Prairie Ice—with the ultimate goal of joining the Major Women's Hockey League. "We would be there next year, if we had the money," said West. "The talent's already pretty good." The team was composed mainly of alumni of both the University of Regina and the University of Saskatchewan, and practised over the winter, playing its first tournament over the Christmas season. In the meantime, West turned to a spot behind the bench. She coached a midget team in Regina and liked it, although at times getting her ideas across took some patience. "It's frustrating at times. It's very hard to go back and break things down for players," she said. Her education helps her address these challenges.

West's experience as a coach had her looking at options at a higher level. "I was kind of throwing resumes out to any job which came up in the CIS (formally CIAU)," she said, adding that she hoped her interest would open a door over the next five years. Then Laurier University called over Christmas of 2003 and she headed east for a three-month trial. "I thought about it for three days and decided to try it, see if I liked it, and what I could learn," she said. At the time of this interview, she liked coaching at the university level, but added that she was not sure she wanted to give up playing for the commitment of coaching full-time. "Once you get into coaching at a level like this, it's kind of hard to play," said West. "It's hard to go out to practice and know you're not really part of it as a player."

The Tiger Had Claws

Dave "Tiger" Williams earned a reputation in hockey as a rough and ready forward who never backed down from anybody on the ice. In fact, he was often an instigator of fisticuffs, but he was also the type of character who endeared himself to his teammates and to his fans. Over an NHL career spanning 962 games in the National Hockey League, he racked up 3,966 penalty minutes—an NHL record that remains standing long after Williams' retirement following the 1987–88 season. For those without easy access to a calculator, the record means he spent more than 66 complete games in NHL penalty boxes. Williams would also play in 83 NHL playoff games with another 455 PIMs, meaning he essentially missed 7.5 of those games in the box.

Williams makes no apologies for his style. He said he knew his role and was willing to play the way he was expected to in order to hold his place in the NHL for so many seasons. He likened the situation to an old rhyme he heard ages ago. "I came into the league a crusher. One night I thought I was a rusher, and the next night I was an usher," he recites. It was a philosophy he worked by. "You do what you do best, and you don't try to change that." If one thing set Williams' career apart from the majority of tough customers, it was that he played that way right until the end of his career. In his last full season—his second last—in Los Angeles, he had 358 PIMs. "Not many guys play the way I played as long as I did," he said. "I stayed in my role straight through. I didn't wander off on the yellow brick road."

Williams was born in Weyburn in 1954, starting his road to the NHL on the nearby river. "We started as soon as we were old enough to stand up on skates on the Souris River in Weyburn." At about six, he started playing organized hockey. "Being a typical prairie guy, I played hockey all winter, had a break in spring, and then played baseball all summer." A developmental break occurred for Williams when he played on a team of 12- and 13-year-olds who played midget-aged competition. "We had to play against bigger and stronger kids, and they were faster, too," he said. It made the younger players improve their skills to compete. "You develop more when you get to play at higher levels." It helped, too, that Williams, as a midget-aged player, came under the coaching of Dwight McMillan, who would go on to an outstanding career as coach of the Saskatchewan Junior Hockey League Weyburn Red Wings, where he reached the 900-win plateau in 2004. Williams said McMillan had a simple coaching style that in many ways stuck throughout his career. "He had a fairly simple philosophy—go out and work as hard as you can, and don't leave anything behind."

As a youth, Williams said he used his greatest asset to best advantage on the ice. "When I was growing up in Weyburn, I was at best an average player. The only edge I had was that I was as strong as anybody and I could look after myself." Williams' work ethic lifted him to the Western Hockey League's Swift Current

Broncos, a team that saw five players drafted, with four making it to the NHL and the fifth to the World Hockey Association. It helped that Stan Dunn, formerly of Weyburn, was with the Broncos the year Williams tried out. "Again, that was a big break for me. He knew who I was, so that helped out," he said. Dunn also took Williams' career a step further, too. "Stan was a wonderful guy. He was a lot like Dwight McMillan. He made you into a better man before he made you into a better hockey player."

Williams said it's important for players to come under the guidance of good people as they progress in the game, something he said he had as a youngster. "All through my minor hockey and junior hockey, I never had a bad coach. I never had a coach who wasn't a wonderful person," he said. "As a young man it's so important to have good people around you. That getting off on the right foot is so important to a young man."

Williams said his days in Swift Current are still some of his best hockey memories. "I can remember every single guy like it was yesterday," he said. Even today when he participates in benefit games with other former NHLers, they end up talking about their junior days as much as their pro days. The closeness comes from the players having the same focus, that of graduating to the next level of the game. "We all knew if we don't win, we don't get exposed to the scouts," he said, adding that catching a scout's eye was the only avenue to the pros.

Obviously, Williams developed as a hockey player and caught some eyes, to the point he was drafted in the second round of the 1974 NHL draft, 31st overall, by Toronto. He also went in the WHA draft to the Cincinnati Stingers, 33rd overall. Going into the draft year, Williams said he fully appreciated how critical the event was in the sense of fulfilling hockey dreams. "If you don't do it, then you don't get another chance to get drafted." Often it comes down to the inner fire to succeed, as much as skill in the game, and that was what Williams relied on, although in his last two seasons in Swift Current he eclipsed the 1,200-point plateau both times.

Much of the inner desire was a natural flair for the rougher side of the game. Williams said most people would suggest it just came naturally to him, and they might be right. "When you wrestled with five brothers every day of your life, the older ones knocking the stuffing out of you, and you practising on the younger ones, I guess it was sort of natural," he said. That being said, having 52 goals in his last year of junior was an assured ticket to the draft. "If you scored 50 goals in junior you were going to get drafted."

Going to Toronto was a bonus. "I was a big-time Toronto fan. We used to go to a neighbour's house to watch the hockey games because we didn't have a TV." The summer of the draft, Williams got married, his honeymoon a crisscrossing of Canada and the United States paid for by both Toronto and Cincinnati as they made their pitches to sign the rookie. In Toronto, he was met at the airport by King Clancy and attended races at Woodbine Racetrack sitting in Conn Smythe's private boxes. After visiting both cities, Williams headed to Chicago to decide which contract to accept. His new father-in-law said to do what he deemed best. His own father had a more pointed view of the situation. "I called Dad. He said, 'You stupid little moron, I can't watch you on TV in Cincinnati, but I can if you are in Toronto,'" said Williams.

The Leafs were the eventual choice, with Clancy and Johnny McClelland flying into Chicago to have the deal signed, which was for $125,000. "Dad hadn't made that kind of money in his whole lifetime." While they courted Williams hard, once his signature was on the contract, the Leafs weren't exactly in regular contact with the young prospect. "That whole summer after I signed my contract, I never got one phone call. I never got a program for conditioning or anything." Once at the Toronto camp, Williams quickly learned that it was going to be a big step to the NHL, especially with some 200 hopefuls in attendance as the camp began. "I don't know why they called it a training camp. It was a bloody war." To begin camp, the young players never even saw a puck, instead skating sprints for hour-and-a-half sessions.

Williams' career with the Leafs, and his reputation as a fighter, didn't start smoothly. He lost a fight handily to tough guy Keith Magnuson, "and the next day they sent me down (to Oklahoma) ... Then again I had another break," he said. Mike Sauter, from Wawota, had played in Weyburn and was now captain in Oklahoma. As a stick boy years earlier, Williams had gotten to know Sauter. "I looked up to him when I was 12 years old, and I still looked up to him." Sauter helped the young forward fit into the role for which he was to become famous. Eddie Shack, the resident tough guy in Toronto, was injured, and Williams again got a break, being called up to fill the void. In his first game back with the Leafs, Williams had three fights, excelling in each one. "Mr. (Harold) Ballard said, 'Kid, call your wife. We're keeping you.'"

"It was a case of taking the opportunity as it presented itself," said Williams. "When opportunity knocks, you've got to grab it by the throat and strangle it." With the word of Leaf owner Ballard, Williams was a Leaf for the next six seasons. It was a dream come true, considering it was with the team he had watched as a youth on the old black and white TV. Williams lived out the dream up until 53 games into the 1979–80 season, when he was sent across Canada to the Vancouver Canucks. It was a deal that still angers him. The anger was focussed on the Leafs' general manager at the time. "I wasn't happy. If I'd ever got my hands on Punch Imlach I'd have ripped his esophagus out of his throat and stomped on it," he said.

As much as he hated the move—in part because the Canucks

had so little tradition to draw on compared to Toronto—it would be in Vancouver that Williams came closest to a Stanley Cup. The Canucks went to the finals in 1982. That they didn't win—Williams was never on a Cup-winning team—is his greatest hockey regret. "There were a lot of great players I played with and against that never got it," he said. "But there was a vacuum … At times, like when I'm waiting for a moose to come out so I can shoot it, I find myself thinking it would have been nice to have won a Stanley Cup."

Yet Williams said the desire for a Cup has to be weighed against a career he is proud of, too. "I had a great career. When you get out of the NHL you'll never do anything else that will come anywhere near fulfilling what you just left." Williams said just playing in the NHL is an achievement players should appreciate. "Only one percent of us who lace on a pair of skates in a rink or the backyard ever get to do it, even for one game."

The Yin and Yang of the Yorkton Terriers

The Saskatchewan Junior Hockey League has a history stretching back more than three decades. Sitting at the top of the league's all-time records list are two players who skated with the Yorkton Terriers franchise. One player is in the record books for his skills around the net. The other is there for his willingness to bend and break the rules governing the game.

Darrell Spelay spent four seasons baffling goaltenders in the SJHL, scoring 243 goals and adding 208 assists for 451 points in 246 games played. The points total is the best in the SJHL's history, 48 points better than Greg Thomson, also a former Terrier and a linemate of Spelay's. Spelay's 243 goals is also a league record. Spelay's 451 points aren't bad stats for a guy who started in minor hockey as a goaltender. "One of my minor coaches said I was too good a skater to be a goalie," said Spelay, whose jersey is retired by the Terriers. So he moved to the wing and found what he termed a natural scoring touch.

The long-time record is something of a surprise to Spelay some 20 years later. "I guess I am a little surprised," he said. That being said, he added that hockey has changed, too, to the point that few players last four years in the SJHL now, either advancing to the Western Hockey League or a college scholarship before they play as 20-year-olds. "Players playing four years in the SJ are almost a thing of the past," he said, which helps protect his record, although he added, "records are made to be broken, too." While admitting he had a knack for potting goals, Spelay was not taking all the credit for his success. "I was just fortunate to play with some excellent players who were able to get me the puck," he said with a smile. "There were a lot of empty net tip-ins created by great playmakers."

Two of the set-up men who remained fresh in Spelay's mind were Brian Kuspira and Greg Thomson. "They were absolutely essential. I think if you look at every goal I scored, one of those guys, if not both, would have had an assist on it. You're only as good as the guys around. Hockey is a team game." Spelay still sees Kuspira regularly, since both still live in Yorkton, and he talks with Thomson, who has been in Germany where he headed to play hockey, at least once a year, maintaining ties to his two linemates.

When it came to physical play, and in particular dropping gloves for some fisticuffs, Grant Ottenbreit was the man, amassing 1,329 penalty minutes, seven more over his career than Kelly Klippenstein of the Weyburn Red Wings. Ottenbreit said hockey was always his passion. "I never played a whole lot of other sports. Hockey was the one I played. It was my one sport and I loved it. Before school, after school, on weekends, I was always at the shinny rink." As a youngster, Ottenbreit patrolled the blue line, but as a junior with the Terriers, he was quickly moved to the wing, where he assumed the role of enforcer on the team. It was a case of recognizing his own limitations as a player and having a willingness to do whatever he had to do to play as a Terrier. Even with that, Ottenbreit said he was lucky to make the team in the fall of

1984. It was a season the Terriers were in a massive rebuilding program—they won only eight of 64 games in his rookie season. "There were no good veterans at all. The only reason I made the team was because there were no strong vets," he said.

In his first training camp, Terrier general manager Max Chambers set out Ottenbreit's role, if he was going to make the team. "He just kept me around to fight," he said. He had no problem stepping into the role. "I'd do anything to make the team ... I'd have carried all the guys' bags and taped their sticks just to play. Look at the alternatives to hockey—going to school or going to work."

Spelay also started with the Terriers in a season the team was retooling. However, the gifted forward would stand out for the young team. For the 1979–80 season, Spelay would earn Most Valuable Player honours from the Terriers. He scored 56 goals and led the team with 86 points, which was second in the league. The same season, he earned the team's Most Sportsmanlike Player award. As for the MVP award following the 1979–80 season, Spelay said he never viewed it as too big an event in his career. "I've never been one for personal accolades ... Everybody had their jobs to do. There's no 'I' in team," he said. For Spelay, it was only one outstanding season in a four-year Terrier career that would rank him among the best players ever to skate for the team.

When the Yorkton Terriers held a fan vote to name the All-Millennium team in 2000, it was Spelay who led the way. Spelay was the top vote-getter in fan voting with 880, securing his spot on right wing. It was an honour that followed the retirement of his sweater and an induction into the Yorkton Sports Hall of Fame as a member of the SJHL winning team. "I owe the Terrier organization a whole bunch for those honours," he said, adding that he is now trying to give something back to the team, having joined the executive in the spring of 2003. When he was chosen for the Millennium team, Spelay said, "My very first year we had one veteran on the team, Bob Burak. It took us some time to get a feel for the league."

Becoming a fighter, a protector of teammates, was an easy step for Ottenbreit, in that it fit his style. "I was always kind of a rugged kid. I always played rough on the snow hill or tackle football with the older kids." Ottenbreit said that in his era, the role of a fighter was certainly more pronounced, although there remains a role today, too. "If you're down three goals, you might need something to help turn it around. Or if you're up three goals, you need someone to respond when they look to turn it around." In his day, Ottenbreit said he was also more of a bodyguard, especially for goaltenders, who were more often run in his day. "You have to step in then. That happened a lot back then, but you don't see it anymore." It's not a case where Ottenbreit won every fight; he guesses he won maybe only 15 percent, holding his own among the majority and losing his share. However, he said winning was not as important as accepting the challenge and standing up for the team.

While noted as something of a pugilist on skates, by his final year with the Terriers Ottenbreit was on the team's top line along with Mark Marianchuk and Ed Zawatsky. Zawatsky would amass 152 points that season, still a Terrier season record. "I'd worked on my game quite a lot the first two years trying to improve," Ottenbreit said, adding that while he never became a great skater, his passing and positional play did improve. Of course, he credited his linemates with the success offensively. "Those guys were so talented. I was just there to babysit. I made things more comfortable for them. They felt better when I was there," he said, adding with a laugh, "They had really good years because I played with them. They would probably have had really great years if I hadn't."

Ottenbreit said knowing his record still stands surprises him, but he said it's a case where he played three seasons in the league, whereas others may have racked up huge penalty minutes in a single season, but didn't stay long in the SJHL. Regardless of how he reached the record, it's one he looks back on with pride. "I am proud of it. There was no way I was going to set records by scoring goals and I wasn't a goaltender," he said. "You don't want to teach a young kid to fight all the time, but there are roles in hockey and they have to be filled."

After his record-setting days with the Terriers, Ottenbreit would spend three seasons in the East Coast Hockey League, and he even had a tryout with the former Winnipeg Jets of the National Hockey League, a run he simply termed "a lot of fun." "I would do it all over in a heartbeat. There's nothing like playing hockey in your hometown. You run the risk of being a dog some days, but overall you get treated pretty good."

The numbers Spelay put up as a Terrier almost saw him leave to go to the Western Hockey League and the Brandon Wheat Kings. "My third year was the closest. I went to the Brandon Wheat Kings camp. I went down just for the experience," he said. Spelay led the Wheat Kings in scoring through training camp and returned to Yorkton with the idea of getting some more clothes and heading back to Brandon. "I had a good camp. I was leading the team in exhibition scoring. I was told I had made the team." But instead of returning to Brandon, Spelay chose to stay with the Terriers, thanks in part to the influence of then-Terrier coach Gerry James. "He told me if I was that good, I could be drafted right out of the SJHL," said Spelay in an interview at the time of his Millennium selection. "It's the one thing I'd change," he admitted, but he doesn't blame James. "It was my decision in the end."

Still, James is a coach Spelay admired. "Having James as a coach was a bonus to anyone who played for him at the time," said Spelay. "He was like a second father to you." Spelay said people need to remember they were only teenagers at the time, with paths to choose from that included not only hockey, but fast cars, girls, and other distractions from the game. James helped the players through it by knowing what motivated them to play hockey. "He knew what buttons to push for Darrell Spelay to turn it up a notch," said Spelay.

Today, he stills wonders what might have happened had his decision been different. "If I had it to do over again, I may have made a different decision," he said again. "Now when I look back upon it, maybe I didn't give it the 100 percent effort I should have." Spelay said that in the era he played in, there were players being drafted into the National Hockey League from the SJHL, but he might have pushed his career further. But as his Terrier career ended, Spelay ended up only travelling as far as Langenburg to play senior hockey with the Warriors. He said he never really considered going farther. "I still loved hockey, but I had no interest at that time," he said. "I look at it now and ask myself the question. But then I didn't feel like moving on. It was my own decision. I don't feel sour about it a bit."

That's one big difference he sees in junior hockey today. Players are leaving home at younger ages to play midget and junior, and are more at ease with such moves. "The philosophy behind the game has changed," said Spelay. "They are used to making a lot of critical decisions early in life." Considering his path in hockey, Spelay had some advice for today's players. "Don't ever sell yourself short," he said.

No Singing the Blues for Federko

For 13 years Bernie Federko toiled in the National Hockey League, leading the St. Louis Blues for more than a decade. Twelve years after retiring, following one season in Detroit, Federko was named to the Hockey Hall of Fame. He said the induction was beyond belief. "That is probably the absolute pinnacle any player can get (to) as an individual," he said. While a Stanley Cup is the goal of every NHL player, Federko said achieving such success relies on many factors, including team ownership and management being willing to build a contending team, and a healthy dose of luck. But making the Hall of Fame is an award marking an individual's success in the league. "It was such a huge thrill to be honoured with the elite of the league," he said. "It's the most flattering, humbling thing that you can achieve. It absolutely floors me to think about it."

There was a time Federko wasn't sure the call from the Hall of Fame would come, but he feels he deserved the induction when it came. The announcement was a nice exclamation point on Federko's career. "I'm so honoured," he said. "I always felt I should be there. People who watched me play all thought so, too." Federko said he knows some question his induction, "but to put up numbers like I did ... What was I doing? Doing it with mirrors?"

While in retrospect Federko was looking forward to the Hall of Fame, he admitted that, as a youngster, his dream never went beyond just making the NHL. "I never really looked at myself in that way back then," he said. "I'm very proud of what I did ... But I never dreamed of having that (his induction) ever happen. It was after I retired and people said, 'Hey, look at his numbers,' that's when you start thinking about it."

In the summer of 2002, just prior to his official induction, Federko returned to Foam Lake, Saskatchewan, the place of his birth, to be honoured by his hometown. That too was a special, career-capping moment. "That's where my roots are. It's always nice when you're honoured by the people of your hometown. Foam Lake is where I got my opportunity." Federko still lives in St. Louis, and he said he has grown to appreciate the opportunity he had as a kid, playing hockey in a small town. While his three sons played hockey, it was up to a parent to drive them to every game and practice. When he was young, he said, "We walked to the rink. We could just walk down the street, strap them on (skates), and play for hours and hours."

While in Foam Lake for the 2002 event, which honoured him along with fellow Foam Lake-born NHLers Dennis Polonich and Pat Elynuik, Federko reflected on his youth. "The rink used to be across from our house. Then it burned down," recalled Federko, sitting in the hallway leading from the ice surface to the dressing room of the new Foam Lake rink, where he played through midget hockey. "I played midget hockey here and with the senior Flyers team at the same time," he said, adding that he was only 16 at the time. Federko said leaving home to play midget was never really a consideration. "I could have gone to Yorkton, Estevan,

Weyburn. They were all calling," he said. "Mom and Dad just said no." A year later he was a member of the Saskatoon Blades of the Western Hockey League. "I had two older brothers going to college in Saskatoon, so it helped," he said.

While Federko had shown flashes of his talent in Foam Lake, he said he began to believe he had a career in hockey in his second season with the Blades. "I led the team with about 100 points (107). I think then was when I knew I was going to get drafted," he said. "I knew I had a chance to play in the NHL." It was in Saskatoon that he also met coach Jack McLeod. "He was the best junior coach you could probably ever have. He knew the systems of hockey so well ... To me junior is where you learn to become a professional hockey player. When I turned pro, I think I knew as much about the game as I could (from McLeod)."

Federko said it was a case of recognizing he was on the verge of fulfilling a dream he shared with so many Canadian youth. "I think any kid in this country who has played hockey, their dream is to play in the NHL," he said, adding that kids want to emulate their heroes—in his case former Montreal great Jean Beliveau, whom he would meet years later. "When I first got to meet him I was totally in awe."

Following his third season with the Blades, Federko would be drafted seventh overall by the St. Louis Blues. "It was a thrill, but I was disappointed, too, because I had been told I was probably going to be the first pick," he said. As it turned out, Rick Green went first overall to the Washington Capitals, where he launched a pretty solid career with 845 games and 263 points. However, the same draft saw two of Federko's Saskatoon Blade teammates also go ahead of him, Blair Chapman to Pittsburgh was second overall, and Fred Williams went fourth to Detroit. Chapman would play 402 NHL games and earn 231 points, while Williams would see only 44 NHL games and seven points. After an MVP season with the Blades, Federko said he felt he was the top player in the draft. "I knew I could have helped Detroit, or Washington, or Pittsburgh," he said. Still, Federko said Emile Francis of the Blues showed faith in him. "He (Francis) was my biggest supporter. I was his first round pick after he took over in St. Louis," said Federko. "He believed in me and gave me a chance."

In St. Louis, things didn't go too smoothly at first. Federko arrived at his first camp just in time to have a cast removed from his foot. "I made an ass of myself, because I couldn't skate. I couldn't even turn, it hurt so much," he said. So Federko was sent to Kansas City in the Central Hockey League, where he met coach Barclay Plager. "He took me under his wing," he said. When he was called up in February, he was in the NHL to show. Federko said Plager was an important person in his career. "He was a father figure and a big brother when my family was a thousand miles away. He really encouraged me to excel." In St. Louis, players such as Garry Unger and Derek Sanderson helped Federko fit in. "Turk (Sanderson) knew I was taking his job, but he showed me things like how to take a faceoff," said Federko.

It would be advice Federko would utilize well, earning Rookie of the Year honours in 1976–77, and being chosen for two all-star teams. Over his career, which totalled 1,000 games, he had 369 goals and 1,130 regular-season points. Federko said the 1,000-game plateau just happened to coincide perfectly with his decision to retire. "I went to Detroit my last year, and we didn't even make the playoffs, so I knew there were going to be changes," he said. That likely meant going with youth. While he had a year left on his contract, he felt that to play would mean moving his family yet again, and instead hung up his skates. If he had been short of the 1,000 games, the lure to play another season would have been far greater.

Still, it's a career Federko has a difficult time picking specific moments out of. "I really don't see my career that way," he said. Of course, some moments are remembered by every player, like his first NHL goal past Boston goaltender Gerry Cheevers, and his first game in St. Louis when he scored a hat trick, including the game winner, with only a couple of minutes remaining in the game. "I've had so many fond memories," he said. Federko includes among them two all-star appearances, including his first in 1980, which happened to also be the first all-star appearance of blossoming star Wayne Gretzky and the final all-star appearance of the legendary Gordie Howe. "That was very special," he said, noting that making the all-star roster as a centre was difficult in his era. "I had three years in a row where I scored at least 100 points, and I didn't make the all-star team any of those years," he said. "It's always a very special time when you get to play with the elite of the league."

However, throughout his career, one thing eluded him—the Stanley Cup. "It was a huge disappointment, because that's what your goal is," he said. "Winning a Cup is the ultimate thing there is … I dreamed of holding the Stanley Cup over my head and drinking champagne from it." However, Federko has become a realist about not winning the Cup. "It takes 25 guys to want it to win it," he said. "One guy doesn't have a lot of control over it. It's not an individual game. You need everybody." Skating for St. Louis meant playing in relative NHL obscurity. "Playing in St. Louis, we never had very much press," he said.

Today, Federko is part of that press, as he does colour for television broadcasts of Blues games. "The game is different," he said. "I think the game was more entertaining when I played … but the athletes are better, stronger, faster today. That's evolution. That's training. That's million-dollar contracts." The big dollars today keep players in shape in order to keep the big dollars rolling in. "To us, the game was still a passion. Today, it's much more of a business," he said. But it's a business Federko is still a part of. For eight seasons, he has been a colour commentator on Blues hockey games, the first four years on radio, and now on TV. He said the team called him when they needed a radioman, and he jumped at the opportunity. "The game has been my life. I know the game well," he reasoned. "I know the players. It hasn't been that hard a transition … It was just a great opportunity to do something in the game I grew up with, and played for so long."

Youth No Barrier to Centennial Cup Glory

It was a Cinderella season for the Notre Dame Hounds. The historic school located in the small community of Wilcox had been famous for its sports ever since Father Athol Murray had moved west to establish Notre Dame. In the spring of 1987, the school's AAA Midget Hounds team had gone to the Air Canada Cup final, losing a close one to a team from Quebec. In the fall of the same year, Notre Dame stepped up a level, joining the Saskatchewan Junior Hockey League.

Tim Green was a team member of the Hounds who entered the SJHL, finding almost instant success, although even the players weren't sure how the season might go. "We didn't know," he said. "We knew we had pretty well the same team that went to the Air Canada Cup, but we didn't know what the step up would be like with such a young team." At the same time, having lost in the Canadian Midget Championships did help set a goal for the young Hounds. "I think there was certainly some bitterness there," said Green of the loss. "We expected ourselves that we'd win that final. We just came up short." The disappointment galvanized the young team in junior. "We were a determined hockey bunch," said Green. "We didn't accept losing. We pushed each other … There weren't too many times guys took a night off because of the competition on that team. We just wanted to play well every night."

Stephane Gauvin was in Grade 9 when he moved to Notre Dame, playing two years of bantam, then the midget season with the finals loss and the move up to the SJHL. "I thought it was a pretty big step. It was sure exciting to move up and play junior hockey." At the same time, Gauvin said no one knew what to expect making the jump up a league. "We knew we had talent, but we just wanted to be competitive. After a good dozen games, though, we started to think we could do more." There was a good feeling among the Hounds based on the environment at Notre Dame. "The majority of us had been at the college, playing on the same teams for three or four years," said Gauvin. "It was a very strong family unit. I think that's the biggest reason we had the successes we did. Just the atmosphere in Wilcox is amazing."

Barry MacKenzie, long a fixture of the Notre Dame hockey program, coached the 1988 Hounds, who took the then-Centennial Cup in their first year as members of the Saskatchewan Junior Hockey League. "We were young," recalled MacKenzie. "I had coached most of those kids for one or two years as midgets. I knew what they were capable of, but nobody knew what we would do." The Hounds team that ended up surprising the hockey world was really pushed onto the junior stage when most could have still been playing midget. MacKenzie explained that Notre Dame made the move into the SJHL to give players a hockey option as they concluded their schooling. But in that first year, experienced players were rare. "They were just kids at the time," he said. But what kids they turned out to be. Nineteen team members went on to earn American college scholarships. Among those were Jason Herter, who would be a first-round draft selection of the Vancouver Canucks, and National

Hockey League players such as Scott Pellerin, Joby Messier, Rod Brind'Amour, and Curtis Joseph.

Through the season the wins piled up for the Hounds, but often only by a slim margin or a goal or two. Green said that helped the Hounds build the character to succeed when the play-offs rolled around. "You don't learn a lot when you win by a lot of goals," he said. "We knew we had to compete every night ... You have to play tough competitive hockey."

Looking back at 1988, MacKenzie said one of the toughest series for the Hounds came in the SJHL playoffs against the Yorkton Terriers, coached by Dennis Polonich and led on the ice by sniper Perry Fafard. "Perry Fafard was a really excellent player," said MacKenzie. "It was a tough series. I think we won it in six." Gauvin said the Terriers proved a difficult hurdle. "They were coming on toward the end of the season. Dennis Polonich, he had them playing hard. I think he urged everything he could out of them." Fafard also drew his opponent's respect. "He was so fast," he said, adding that the two still occasionally face off in teacher games, as both are in education in Moose Jaw. "I still can't catch him," he quipped. The Terriers may have been a key for the Hounds' playoff successes ahead. "It was probably a blessing we had a tough series with them, in retrospect," said Gauvin.

In the ANAVET Cup with Manitoba's top team, the Winnipeg South Blues, the Hounds again took the series in short order, sweeping it in four, setting up the series of the season with the Alberta/B.C. champions from Calgary. It was another scare for the Hounds. Calgary jumped to a 3–1 lead in the series, putting the Hounds on the brink of elimination for the first time. It was time for a look inward for the players, who decided. "We hadn't put our best foot forward," said Green, who added they believed a full effort would still win them the series. "Everybody was on the same page."

"No doubt it was a tough series. We were down 3–1 and pretty well everybody had us written off," said MacKenzie. The Hounds pulled off a game five win in Notre Dame after MacKenzie "gave them some emotional stuff to get them ready." Gauvin credits MacKenzie for the turnaround, with his talk prior to Game 5. "He said, 'You guys could fold the tent and still be considered heroes. You're just a bunch of midget players, but why would you want to stop here?'" said Gauvin. In Game 5 "we came out just possessed," he said, winning 7–2. However, going back to Calgary for Games 6 and 7, the Canucks still seemed in control. But Notre Dame won Game 6, allowing the Hounds to play a trump card, the support of an entire school for game seven. "We loaded up the whole school and bused them to Calgary," said MacKenzie. "They had one end (of the rink) for us. It was a real boost for our kids to see all the red faces (the Hound colour)." School president Martin Kenny had arranged to bus the entire student body to the game. Gauvin said the effect was even felt in the dressing room before the pre-game skate. "You could hear them stamping their feet. It was just like the rink was shaking. That was a real motivator, not that you need a lot of extra motivation in a Game 7."

"It was pretty nice to have them there. We knew we had to buck up there and win it for them," said Green. The Hounds would lead the game 3–2, when Calgary was awarded a penalty shot with two seconds left on the game clock. "You can't describe the feeling of watching a penalty shot that could have tied the game," said Green, adding there was unimaginable relief when Joseph stopped Dean Larsen on the shot. "It would have been a huge turning point in the game." Gauvin said Joseph was the hero, not only for the penalty shot save, but an acrobatic one earlier in the period. "He (Joseph) was out of position. He dove over with his stick and stopped it. I was backchecking my man. I had stopped skating, conceding the goal, so I could see the stop. It was amazing." When the game buzzer sounded, "it was just mayhem. It was just wild," said Green.

The celebration was tempered for the Hounds, who knew one more challenge lay ahead, the Centennial Cup Tournament as the top Tier II junior team in Canada. Gauvin said the emotion of the win could have been too much for them to be ready for the Centennial Cup, but MacKenzie was again the settling force. "You've got to credit Barry MacKenzie with getting us back and focussed and ready." MacKenzie said the national championships are pressure filled, thanks to every game being critical. "In a seven-game series you can play a couple of bad games and get into a bit of trouble and still bounce back," he said. "In a long series you can get over the nerves." In a situation where a single loss can mean elimination, MacKenzie said teams must stay within a game plan. "You just can't allow slippage of discipline. Players have to be performing to their full potential at all times." That was MacKenzie's philosophy, one that saw the Hounds defeating Lloydminster 7–2 in their championship season, only to end up with a post-game skate. "I told them they may have won, but you didn't play well … I want my team to play hard all the time," MacKenzie said.

Going into the championship, the Hounds weren't exactly picked to win. "I still think they figured Pembroke (the host team) was the team to beat. They had two or three college players who had come back to play," said MacKenzie. "So they had two or three pretty mature hockey players who would lead them." In round robin action, the Hounds lost in overtime to Pembroke, but it was a loss that left MacKenzie feeling good. "They really relied on about two lines at the most. I knew if we kept going with our commitment and dedication to the game and using four lines we would do all right." In semi-final action, the Hounds prevailed 6–3 over Pembroke.

With the win, Gauvin said he started to feel as though the

Hounds would triumph. "It seemed like Pembroke was the biggest obstacle," he said. The Hounds would still advance to the finals against Halifax, dropping behind 2–1 after 40 minutes. In the dressing room, Green recalled the team still being confident. "I remember sitting there saying, 'We can do it. Second is not an option.'" Gauvin said the tough series against the Terriers and the emotional win over Calgary steeled the team enough that a one-goal deficit with a period to go was not a concern. "At that point there was so much behind us we weren't going to concede defeat." In the end, the Hounds' depth would win it all, with Dwayne Norris scoring the winner in the final on a set-up from future NHLer Brind'Amour.

Norris would score the game winner in Canada's gold-medal victory in the 1990 World Junior Championships as well. The national championship was like a fantasy fulfilled. "We had played 92 games that season," said Green. "We had fulfilled a dream, our goal. You can't put words to the feeling."

"It was just pure joy," said Gauvin, adding he feels more appreciation for the excitement exhibited by teams hosting the Stanley Cup now. He added that the win remains the best moment of his hockey days, in fact calling the whole season "the best year of his life." MacKenzie credits that edition of the Hounds as the best he has been involved with. "Just because of the level of play we had—the hurdles you had to go through to get to the Centennial Cup," he said.

And then there was the Joseph factor. Now a dominant force in net in the NHL, back then he was often the difference for the Hounds. "Those were the days of the shootout," said MacKenzie. "We won a lot of games on the basis of the shootout." That and a deadly power play, thanks to Brind'Amour and others. "Our power play allowed us to play our game. Even though we were young, they couldn't goon us because of the strength of our power play," said MacKenzie.

As for why the Hounds were successful in 1988 and no SJHL team would be again until the 2003 Humboldt Broncos brought home the renamed Royal Bank Cup, MacKenzie said in part it's due to the quality of the league. "We almost beat up on ourselves. It's hard getting out of our league because we are so competitive," he reasoned. "There's no nights where you are assured a win ... Even the fifth- and sixth-place teams can knock you off on any given night. It's a grind."

Team Delivers Long-Coveted Cup to Town

I t was the season Theodore Buffalos players and fans had dreamed of for nearly two decades. In March 2003, the Buffs accomplished something 16 previous editions of the team had not managed—they captured the Fishing Lakes Hockey League championship. And the Buffalos did it in style—winning 10 straight playoff games. The Buffalos defeated Springside three straight in their best-of-five opening series, then took three straight over Wadena in the semi-finals. In the final, it was a four-game sweep over Kelliher in the best-of-seven series by scores of 7–4, 3–0, 6–4, and 7–5.

"It's going to take a few days for it to sink in, I think," said Buffs coach Dick Onslow in an interview after clinching the title. For Onslow, it was a huge win, since he had been with the team for nearly a decade. The team made it to the final two seasons ago, but lost to Foam Lake, but the win was worth the wait. "This year we had a lot of depth," he said. Onslow said the team was a solid mix of ex-junior players such as Darren Wilson, Chad Korczak,

Jason Houston, and Trevor Secundiak, with local stalwarts such as Jeff and Jerald Sperling. "We worked on getting each player to make sure we had the right blend," said Onslow. "We started to work on this team in the summer. We had to bring the right players in." And it worked. Onslow said the Buffs had a special chemistry. "The players were just like a family both on and off the ice," he said. "We all had roles on the team. Some guys put the puck in the net and some guys played defence."

Darren Wilson was a role player who excelled at putting the puck in the net. Wilson received the FLHL Most Valuable Player award, doing it with panache by scoring 51 goals and making 57 assists for 108 points. It was a new record for the FLHL. It was a near-fantasy season for Wilson—the kind a player only dreams about. A 108-point season isn't a bad season even in the National Hockey League, but the kicker for Wilson is that he amassed the 108 points in only 24 games, for a smidge better than a 4.5-point-a-game pace. "It was an excellent season," said Wilson in a 2002 interview, following an 11-1 playoff victory for the Buffs that eliminated the expansion Springside Flyers from the opening round of the FLHL playoffs in three straight games. Wilson was modest about the achievement that saw him receive the league's top scorer and Most Valuable Player awards from FLHL president Ron Horvath.

Wilson quickly shared the credit for his success with linemates Lee Poncelet and Dan Cross. "My linemates and I just knew where each other were this year. We got each other the puck well and had a great season," said Wilson. Asked to delve a little deeper into a 108-point season that was some 20 points better than the runner-up in league scoring over the regular season, Wilson said everything just seemed to go right all season. "I just try to find open ice and get in the right place when the puck's around," he said. "I like the offensive part of the game. I was in the right spot at the right time, I guess. It was a good team effort. I just happened to get the puck in the net and got the assists. Our team was amazing all season. It all bonded at the beginning of the season, and went from there."

The 108 points appears to be a league record for a 24-game schedule, said Wilson, bettering the old mark of 107 established by Wynyard's Ryan Peterson two seasons ago. "I'm really surprised that I did it. I didn't think I'd get 108," said Wilson. "When I got to the mid-90s with four games left, I was informed 108 was within reach." However, it took a storybook ending to the season for Wilson to break the record. He entered the final game of the season against Preeceville with 100 points. "I got eight points in the last game to break it," said Wilson, who added it was his best single game of the year. "I have to give my teammates credit for that, too. Every time I was near the net they gave me the puck."

While teammates drew a lot of praise, Wilson also gave kudos to his employer in Yorkton, R. Miller's Plumbing, who he said was always willing to let him sneak away a little early if he needed to attend practice with the Buffs, or get to a game—an often forgotten aspect of hockey's survival. "He (his employer) is excellent when it comes to sports," he said.

Wilson, a Yorkton native who played his minor hockey, including AAA Midget, with the then-Yorkton Mallers, before a stint in Neepawa of the Manitoba Junior Hockey League, was in his third season of senior hockey with the Buffs. At 23, he said he keeps playing for a love of the game. "I just like the game," he said. "I like playing and it's a good group of guys ... I don't regret a minute of it."

While Wilson's success was a big part of the Buffs year, the championship was the ultimate prize. For others on the Buffs, being part of the community is being part of the team. Jerald Sperling and the Theodore Buffalos have become nearly synonymous. He first started with the senior team as a 15-year-old and remained a regular through the championship win at 28. What keeps a dairy farmer—who often does not see home following a Buffalo game until well past midnight, yet must rise for 6 a.m. milking—playing hockey? "I guess it's the enjoyment of the game and the camaraderie of the guys," he said in a 2001 interview. With a herd of dairy cows needing attention every day, the threat of injury is a known factor of the game for Jerald Sperling. "I have a little knee injury right now, so it's always a concern. I've never really had a problem before, but when I start getting older and start breaking down," he said, his voice trailing off a little, then adding, "or maybe it's just bad luck."

"The toughest thing about senior hockey is everybody has to work the next day." Jerald Sperling reminds us that it's a case of local players toiling for the love of the game and not financial reward. However, the championship was a reward all players could appreciate, especially the long-time Buffs. For Jeff Sperling, the championship was the crowning accomplishment of a 12-year career with his hometown team. Sunday morning, Jeff Sperling was exhausted from the partying after the win, but still floating on cloud nine, too, knowing how huge an accomplishment the win was for the team and community. "Some guys said it was 20 years ago since we had won a championship," he said, which would take it back to the era when the team played in the long-defunct Bates Hockey League. "It's been an awful, awful long time."

The final moments of Saturday's win, played on Foam Lake ice because Kelliher did not have ice, are etched in Jeff Sperling's mind. "To be honest, with 2:46 left, I was on the bench, and I looked at the trainer and I had tears in my eyes," he said. "I was on the ice with a minute left. I had the puck with nine seconds left. It was in my hand with four seconds left. I was just hoping I wouldn't get a penalty for gloving the puck." The puck is still in Jeff Sperling's possession, as is his long-time Buffs sweater. "I grabbed my sweater. It was my last night and I took it home." Jeff Sperling said the emotion was intense. "It was just about like winning the Stanley Cup. I really don't know what that's like, but it's the next best thing."

Tom Vosper had retired from senior hockey, but was coaxed back this year after sitting out last season. He said the Cup was likely unfinished business. "Finally it's done," he said in almost relieved fashion Sunday. "That's the end of this chapter ... Now I can ride off into the sunset happy." Vosper said that from the outset of the season, he felt the players were assembled to get the job done. "We had our minds on the league championship for sure," he said.

Still, he put together an award-winning year. The veteran defenceman was named the league's best blueliner through the regular season. "That was a shock. I'm not sure how that worked out," he said. "I was just happy going off the ice after each shift having not been scored on ... but it was an honour." As for the championship win, Vosper said the final game was a tough one. "Kelliher, it was the strongest game they'd played all series," he said, adding that even leading 4–1 after two periods, the game was uncertain. "In the third period we knew they weren't going to lie down. We didn't get fancy. It was just dump it up and chase until it was over." Vosper termed the final buzzer simply "a relief" for him.

The championship ended Vosper's senior hockey days, too, adding that he owes it to his family to spend time with them. He said that stepping out of retirement was a commitment taking him back to the rink away from his first child, and the second who arrived as the season progressed. "My wife was very good about it. She knew this was what I wanted," he said. "Now I'll be at peace with myself."

It was also a victory for longtime Buffalo fans. "I would think there were 150 fans there—at least that many," said Jeff Sperling. "Our old bus, it was just standing room only. The fans were unbelievable." Onslow said Theodore was clearly behind the team. "The whole community was behind us. It was a win for the whole community," he said.

So what was the secret to a season where the Buffalos lost only three regular-season games on their 24-game schedule, and then went 10–0 in the playoffs? "The secret to 10–0 is definitely the character, the morale in the dressing room, and the depth of different kinds of players," said Jeff Sperling. "It was 20 guys sitting in the dressing room that you wouldn't know that they weren't all brothers. We were just that tight. Everybody just loves each other. It was an unbelievable feeling." After drinking the champagne, the team gathered in a circle in the dressing room. "We all had our arms around each other, drinking beer and singing. I looked around and every guy was smiling and laughing. Even the guys who never said anything were laughing."

Once the playoffs began, the Buffs just built one game on the next. "You sniff the Cup and you do that much more to get there," said Jeff Sperling. "We were there when we had to be." He said the team had confidence in its abilities, even on occasions when they had a bad period, or two. "We always knew come the final buzzer we'd be there," he said. "No one ever thought at any time we weren't going to win."

Onslow said he could feel the desire with the team. "With all the depth and character on this team, we couldn't accept losing," he said.

Jeff Sperling said his hockey career is complete, too, just the way he had always wanted it to end. "I wanted to win. I had never won the championship and I wanted to win it once," he said, adding he felt good about the team from the opening day of practice last fall. "I knew everybody. I just felt this year there was a chance to finally win it," he said. Jeff Sperling had hung on to his career in search of the Cup longer than most might have, including two knee scopes this season. "I was going through a bottle of Flexall (liniment) every two games," he said. "Guys would laugh at my two knee braces and liniment and bad shoulder. But carrying the Cup off the ice into the dressing room and drinking champagne from it—that's what it was all about." Jeff Sperling said the win was very much for his parents, too. "If it wasn't for them I probably wouldn't have been there last night," he said. "They were the ones who forced me to get out then when I was four years old. That's when it started, not just last October."

Aboriginal Title Comes to Young Team

Team Saskatchewan won the men's 2003 National Aboriginal Hockey Tournament. It was only the second year the Aboriginal championship for bantam and midget-aged players was held, and the first time a male team from Saskatchewan had taken part. The tournament was played in Ontario at Akwesasne/Cornwall and was only open to teams comprised of players and coaches who were of Aboriginal ancestry. On the male side, only bantam and midget-aged players were allowed.

Barry Sparvier of the Ochapowace First Nation was a member of the championship team, wearing the captain's jersey, as well as leading the team in scoring, with three goals and eight assists for 11 points in the six games played. Sparvier was also named to the male all-star team, along with three other members of the Saskatchewan team, including Craig Morningchild in goal, Justin Magnuson, and Travis Gardipy.

Sparvier said the Saskatchewan team was an interesting mix. While he was the only Saskatchewan Junior Hockey League player, there were others from Junior B, AAA Midget, and AA Midget. "There were lots of personalities," he said. "We had some jokesters and we had some serious guys, but we bonded pretty quickly." As for wearing the "C," Sparvier said it was a great experience. "It was great to be captain and share my experience playing SJ," he said.

Jonas Thomson, who had played his midget hockey in Indian Head that year, said having Sparvier, who was playing with the Yorkton Terriers of the Saskatchewan Junior Hockey League, was a real asset to the team. "He was kind of a leader for us up there coming from junior." The team didn't have a lot of time together before heading to Ontario, but jelled in a hurry. "Everyone knew each other. We'd all played against each other," said Thomson. "We knew we had to work as a team. It didn't take us long to do that—maybe by the end of the first game."

Travis Gardipy from Beardy's First Nation was 16 at the time of the championship, and had been playing with Beardy's Blackhawks in the Saskatchewan AAA Midget Hockey League. He said having the Saskatchewan team in a tournament in Saskatoon a couple of weeks before heading to Ontario was a huge benefit. "We really came together there. It was a time to get our lines together and work on things," he offered.

Charlie Keshane was the team's head coach, and he noted the coaching staff was both surprised and pleased with how the team came together over only a handful of games. "It was surprising how competitive we were in the tournament," he said, but added a loss in the final had some people, including a few of the players, worried they weren't ready for a national tournament. "Even some of the kids weren't too sure they were ready to go to Ontario," he said, adding, "We told them it would take a little while to click."

Justin Magnuson, who also played with Beardy's Blackhawks during the season, said the loss in the tourney final was in retrospect a good thing. "Losing a game in that tournament helped us be better in the future," he said. The team came together in Ontario in a hurry.

Saskatchewan went through the tournament undefeated, winning five straight on the men's side of the draw leading up to the final. "It was tough. There were some tough teams there," said Thomson. "But we just skated hard and worked hard." Magnuson, who hails from Saskatoon, said he felt confident to the point that he expected to go through the tournament without a loss; yet he, too, admitted there were good teams to beat. "Southern Ontario was a good team, very skilled," he offered as an example.

Keshane said again that the coaches were pleased by the results. "We were very surprised we did so well, especially judging from the Saskatoon tournament. But we jelled quite quickly ... They came together so quickly." The coach said a key to the team becoming so close-knit in such a short time was involving the players, not just in practices, but in off-ice activities as well.

The toughest game, though, came in the final, against Manitoba. "They were very good," said Gardipy. "They had quite a few Junior A players on their team." Keshane, too, noted his charges would be in for a tough go in the final game. "They (Manitoba) were the powerhouse there. They had a lot of Junior A and Junior B players. They had a really strong core of hockey players and were defending champs." So going in, Keshane wanted only one thing, "110 percent from the players," and as long as that was there, he would accept either winning or losing.

Sparvier pointed out that it was a game with a weird ending. "That was a crazy game," said Sparvier. "We were down 2–1 with two seconds left." Sparvier said Manitoba thought they had it won until a player grabbed the puck inside the crease area, giving Saskatchewan a penalty shot. Keshane said it was obviously a huge break for Saskatchewan, on a penalty some refs call and others let go. "It was fortunate for us the ref called it." Magnuson said the strange play felt as though the Saskatchewan team was destined to prevail. "I don't know if it was luck or fate. It was probably a bit of both."

With a penalty shot to take, Keshane began looking down the bench for Magnuson, who had had a couple of breakaways in the tournament and done well. But as Keshane looked to centre ice, Gardipy was already standing on the dot. "He had kind of been fighting the puck in the game," said the coach. For his part, Gardipy said he just had a gut feeling he was the one to take the critical shot. "I just went straight to centre ice. I thought I could score," he said, adding that the coaches went with his hunch. "I thought I'd been playing really well throughout the tournament and that I had a chance to score." The confidence Keshane saw in Gardipy's move to centre ice was enough for him. "He was standing at the dot focussing. I thought, he wants it, so let him go. I didn't even watch the play. I turned my head away and waited."

With the gold medal on the line, the young Gardipy just tried to stay focussed on what he had to do. "I just tried to block out all the fans. I was thinking of the move I was going to do on the goalie." Gardipy went in on net, faked once, and shot a forehand along the ice—and the red light went on. "It was relief, and get ready for overtime," he said.

"They had the game won," said Thomson, who noted there were fewer than three seconds on the clock when the penalty was called. Gardipy's goal renewed the team's fire. In overtime, Magnuson was set free on a breakaway less than five minutes in, scoring to give the Saskatchewan team the win. "I just remember I was at the end of my shift. I was a little slow on the backcheck," he said. "I got the puck on a fast breakout." From there it was up to Magnuson, who got past the Manitoba defence, and in on goal.

"I saw the goalie was kind of far back in his net, so I decided to shoot and it went in." Sparvier was also instrumental in the victory, setting up both Saskatchewan's first goal and the overtime winner in the final. "It was fun. I got to do some stuff I never got to before," he added, pointing to his increased offensive role on the team.

Keshane called the game the highlight of his coaching career to that point, adding that the joy he felt was for his young team. In some cases, he said, the players came from isolated communities, and the opportunities to play on the national stage were limited. While some were expected to go on to junior, college, and professional hockey, for "a handful of kids that was the best they would get," he said. For the coaching staff, the training camp might have been the most difficult part of the process, having only three days to select a team. "It was difficult for the staff to come up with a good core of hockey players in such a short time," said Keshane, adding that, fortunately, many players were coming out of competitive midget programs to start with.

Sparvier explained the team held a tryout camp at Beardy's just before Christmas, and he was informed shortly after that he had made the team. Thomson said the tryout was in some ways intimidating, with approximately 100 players in attendance, yet he went into it feeling confident. "I played with and against a bunch of the guys," he said, adding that he'd been told that if he worked hard, he had a good shot at the team. Thomson said coaches told him they liked his speed, aggressiveness, and puck control, three aspects of his game that helped him earn a spot on the team.

For Thomson, who began skating at about three years of age, the tournament was his first time playing hockey outside Saskatchewan. At 17, he said he took that pretty much in stride. "As long as I was playing a sport I liked, it was good. I just wanted to enjoy it while I was there." Looking at the tournament and the championship win, Thomson said it was certainly among the highlights of his hockey career to date. The only thing close to the championship as far as a highlight went was making the Yorkton Terrier roster in the SJHL after their camp in the fall of 2003.

For Gardipy, whose goal breathed life into the team, it was a game to remember. "I think it's one of my biggest moments," he said, adding that playing in the Canada Winter Games in New Brunswick also rated highly. Yet he remembers the gold-medal celebration vividly, too. "We all just jumped on the ice and went crazy. We were all pretty happy with the victory, knowing we had beat a tough team who were defending champions, too."

Sparvier called the Aboriginal crown a definite highlight event. "It was pretty big," he said. "It was my last minor hockey and I went out with a win. And my dad was coaching (an assistant), which made it that much better."

Cup Winner Cherished Memory

With the 1952 Stanley Cup on the line, a boy from Yorkton lived out every hockey player's dream. Metro Prystai scored twice and assisted on the third goal as Detroit won the deciding game of the series 3–0. Prystai would score at the 6:50 mark of the first period, a goal that stood as the Stanley Cup winner. "That year we had a helluva team," said Prystai. "We went through the playoffs and never had a goal scored against us in Detroit." The win was beyond belief in many ways. "It's something you've always dreamed of. You've got to prick yourself to make sure you aren't still dreaming," he said. In 1954, the Wings and Prystai would win the Cup again. "It wasn't maybe quite as exciting as the first," said Prystai. "But that's the name of the game when you're up there, winning the Stanley Cup."

Prystai, born in 1927 in Yorkton, learned to skate and play in the rink of the nearby St. Joseph's Collegiate, and in a rink in the backyard. "And we played a lot of road hockey." When it came time to play the game in a more organized way, Prystai said he was fortunate to come under the guidance of coach Clarence Drake.

"He was really interested in sports. He couldn't skate, but he was still out on the ice in his spats."

At 16, Prystai came to the attention of Scotty Monroe, who was in charge of a midget team in the city. It wasn't exactly love at first sight for Monroe regarding Prystai's skills as a hockey player. "I went out to their camp, but I think they had the team picked before we even went out for it," said Prystai. Then the mumps came along to help the young forward. Enough players on the team were sick that they needed some extra players, and Prystai got a brief shot, one that left Monroe asking where he came from. "Right here in Yorkton. I was at your camp," was Prystai's reply.

The next season, when Monroe moved on to Moose Jaw, the young Prystai was in tow. The move to Moose Jaw was a big one in the early 1940s. "I didn't even know where it was," said Prystai with a laugh. But, billeted with a good family, he settled in rather nicely. On the ice, the team excelled over Prystai's three seasons. "We went to the Memorial Cup two years. The other time we lost in the western semi-final to Edmonton." Emile Francis was in the Moose Jaw nets one season, and Prystai said, "That year we should have gone all the way." However, St. Mike's, the Ontario powerhouse, stood in their way, winning both finals in which Moose Jaw played. "They had a real powerful team," he said, including future Hockey Hall of Fame inductee Red Kelly, who would a few seasons later become Prystai's best friend.

Growing up, Prystai was a diehard Toronto Maple Leaf fan. "We listened to them on the crystal set. We didn't even have a radio. Foster Hewitt would come on. About all we knew was Toronto," he said, pointing to favourite players such as Syl Apps and Charlie Conacher. Given Prystai's affection for Toronto, playing Memorial Cup games at Maple Leaf Gardens was a thrill, one he explained simply as "awesome." Ahead were, of course, more thrills. As a Moose Jaw player, Prystai was signed to a C card by the Chicago Blackhawks of the NHL, the sponsoring franchise. The card earned players $50, which to Prystai was a lot of money. While still 19, Prystai headed to Chicago to his first NHL training camp. He said he recalled walking into Chicago's old Stadium for the camp. Another rookie, Albertan Art Michakuk, who had a dry sense of humour, looked up into the high rafters and remarked, "'Boy, could you put lots of hay in here,'" said Prystai. Heading into the camp, Prystai said he felt good. The Chicago organization had suggested he had a really good shot at making the team. "They were looking for some young players." The Blackhawks may have been seeking youth, but were still anchored by Max and Doug Bentley, and Bill Mosienko. Even with such talent, Prystai said Chicago was not winning on the ice. In three seasons, they failed to make the playoffs, but it was still a good time for Prystai. "I enjoyed it in Chicago. It was a great place to play. The Stadium was just packed with people every game," he said.

Then the deal came. Prystai was home in Yorkton in the summer of 1950 when the news came. "I was looking after the York Lake Golf Course and a taxi came out. There wasn't a phone out there. It took me back in so I could return a call from Jack Adams in Detroit," he said. Adams explained to Prystai that he was now a Red Wing, following a multi-player deal with Chicago. Prystai wasn't thrilled. "I like Chicago. I was just getting used to it there," he told Adams. "But I was happy afterwards. Detroit was a good organization."

Detroit was also talent-laden. They had won the 1950 Stanley Cup and were poised to win three more in short order. The team included future Hall of Famers Gordie Howe, Ted Lindsay, Alex Delvecchio, and Terry Sawchuk. Lindsay and Howe were particularly imposing presences on the ice. "They were good guys to have on your side," said Prystai. "If you got in some trouble they'd be looking after your back. Lindsay especially was a real team player." In the 1954–55 season, Chicago was struggling and Prystai was sent back to the Hawks, almost on loan. While Chicago missed the playoffs, the Wings won yet another Stanley Cup. It was a move that was a bitter pill for the veteran forward, who had settled so well into Detroit.

Partway into the next season, Prystai was moved back to Detroit, playing two more seasons before bad luck struck—twice. "I was playing in Detroit. I took a shot off my ankle," he said. He was sent to Edmonton of the old Western Hockey League to play himself back into shape. A few games into the rehab, Prystai broke his leg. Prystai said he was backchecking and slid into the goal post. "They were almost welded to the ice back then." The net didn't give as the opponent he was checking slid into the leg. He spent nearly six months in a cast. "They sent me to Edmonton again, saying, 'Get in shape and we'll bring you back in,'" said Prystai. However, while the doctor assured him the leg was 100 percent, Prystai said he felt uneasy, but chalked it up to a state of mind. But again, after only a few games, Prystai had the legs knocked out from under him in front of the net. Innocent as the play was, the leg broke again, starting at the same break point, and then fracturing along a different axis. This time he spent about eight months in a cast, during which time he met his wife and decided it was time to hang up the skates.

Prystai's playing days might have been over, but he finished with 151 goals. He has the puck from the 150th versus New York, after Lindsay collected it for him. He had 330 points over 674 regular-season games. His best season was the 1953–53 season, when his 50 points placed him seventh best in the league, and his 34 assists put him fifth in that category. After his career was shortened due to injuries, Prystai turned to coaching, including an ill-fated season in Omaha, where nothing went right. "I was suspended, then reinstated, and fired," he said. He went home to

Yorkton, coaching in both Moose Jaw and Melville, before leaving the game behind.

There are no regrets about hockey for Prystai, who played in a time long before million-dollar contracts. His best year was $10,000. His rookie season, half that. When he had a hometown lawyer helping him do his taxes that first season, Prystai said there was only one question: "You made $5,000 just for playing hockey?" which he said summed up his era pretty well.

Although hockey created the memories, the friendships are what lingered for Prystai. He added that, to this day, more than five decades after his Stanley Cup-winning goal, he still gets Christmas cards and remains friends with players from the old days. Red Kelly, the same guy who led St. Mike's over Prystai's Moose Jaw team in the Memorial Cup, was a best friend. "We lived together in Detroit for seven years," he said. Such friendships were more memorable than most things in his career, and Prystai admits he can't recall his first goal at all.

Brothers on Ice

In some families hockey definitely runs in the blood, and that's certainly the case for the Odelein brothers from Quill Lake—Selmar, Lyle, and Lee. Selmar is the eldest of the trio, born in 1966, lacing up skates at the age of five. It wasn't an experience he would have expected to lead to such notable accomplishments in the sport. "Actually, I didn't like it very much the first couple of times," said Selmar. "I couldn't skate very well and some of my friends could, and I couldn't keep up with them."

While Selmar had to grow into his enjoyment of hockey, his mere presence on the ice helped draw his younger brothers to the game. "Selmar kind of led the way for all three of us," said youngest brother Lyle. "You pretty well followed what your brother did." For Lyle, hockey was something he now recognizes as a cultural love. "In Canada, hockey is always pretty well the first sport," he said. Lyle was like many kids on the prairies, "playing outside until my feet turned purple." Middle brother Lee also commented on the connection between Canadian culture and the game. "Growing up in a small town, that was what you did in the winter."

By the time Selmar was playing atom hockey, he was starting to realize he had talent in the game. When he turned 15, it was time to leave the friendly confines of Quill Lake, a community of about 600 back then, and head to the Saskatchewan capital to play AAA Midget hockey with the Regina Pat Canadians. Regina may not be a major urban centre, but it was still a major change for the young player. "It was tough to leave home more than anything else," he said. "We were a very close family, and I was homesick more than anything." It didn't help that Selmar was billeted in the dorms at Luther College. "There were no more home-cooked meals. It was cafeteria food," he said. "And I didn't have a licence, so most of the time I had to walk to the rink." The mile-and-a-half trek from the dorm to the Agridome may have helped keep him in shape, but it wasn't appreciated. "At the time I wasn't overly pleased with the walk," Selmar said with a laugh. Again, Selmar's lead helped paved the way, as Lyle also headed to Regina at 15 to play with the Pat Canadians. "I was sort of used to it. We'd been driving in and out watching my brother play. So I knew a lot of people when I got there."

As a AAA Midget rookie, Selmar's season wasn't great. "My numbers were nothing much. It was a lot of adjusting to just playing systems and not just playing hockey. It was quite a learning curve my first year," he said. But the following year he blossomed. "I had a real dream season that year," he said. At the major Mac's Midget Tournament in Calgary, he was named the top defenceman. In the Saskatchewan league, he was in the top 10 in scoring from his blue-line position. He was Most Valuable Player in the final round of playoffs against Notre Dame, a series Regina won to advance to the Air Canada Cup tourney in St. Foye, Quebec, where he was a first-team all-star. "It was pretty overwhelming," he admitted, and it was a natural springboard to the Western Hockey League Regina Pats.

In spite of his dominating year at Midget, Selmar said he had no real expectations going up to the next level. "I just wanted to make the Pats." Selmar did more than just make the Pats, he earned back-to-back berths on the national junior team heading to the World Championships. In 1985, it was a gold-medal performance in Helsinki, Finland, and a year later a silver in Halifax, losing to Russia. "Playing in the World Championships would be one of my career highlights," he said. The tournament wasn't quite the showcase then that it has since become. Just the same, on home ice in Halifax, Selmar said the players could feel the expectations. "I really noticed the process for the first time in my life," he said. "It was obviously disappointing not to get the gold." Lyle, too, would head to the famous Mac's Tournament, an opportunity to play in an NHL arena, the only one he set foot in until years later after being drafted by Montreal.

With such a junior career, Selmar could see the National Hockey League draft ahead. "I probably missed a lot of school, meeting with GMs and scouts," he joked. "I realized I was getting pretty close if I could stay healthy." Selmar made the trip to Montreal for the draft alone, his agent being unable to make the trip. On the plane he read a newspaper article saying that he was rated top 10, but wouldn't go until 21st in the first round to Edmonton. "I was a little bit disappointed, but going to the Oilers, I got to play with some of the best players ever," he said.

Selmar said the first time he walked into the Edmonton dressing room was almost indescribable. "It's something you have to experience to understand," he said. The team included the likes of Wayne Gretzky, Jari Kurri, and Mark Messier. He would be 18 when he played his first game. "On my first or second shift, Slats (coach Glen Sather) put me out on the power play. Paul Coffey was my partner," he said, a hint of awe still in his voice.

Lyle would play in the WHL, but moved a few miles south-west, joining the Moose Jaw Warriors. It was there he became a hard-nosed player. He credited his coach Gerry James and the help of Barry Trapp for taking the final steps toward being an NHL-calibre player. "In my last year, James said I wasn't skilled enough to make it on that alone," said Lyle, who added he took that to heart and became more physical. "James and Barry Trapp, they got me on the right page." Lyle played three years with the Moose Jaw Warriors, catching the attention of NHL scouts to the point that Central Scouting had him rated 20th overall for his draft year. However, an injury pushed interest down and Montreal selected him in the seventh round, 141st, in the 1986 draft. "I think the draft is so overrated," he said. "You see more guys taken in the sixth round and later making it than guys in the first five rounds." Lyle said players obviously develop at different rates and some simply show more as juniors, while others go less noticed, are taken in the later rounds, but mature into long-time NHL contributors.

Regardless of where Lyle was chosen in the draft, he was just happy to be selected, a joy made sweeter by the move to Montreal. "It's something you can't even describe," he said of his first time at a Montreal camp. Joining a team with players such as Bobby Smith, Bob Gainey, Larry Robinson, and Patrick Roy was overwhelming, as was simply being at the Montreal Forum. "It was only the second time I'd been in an NHL rink. The first was at the Mac's Tournament with the Pat Canadians."

The camp in Lyle's case was hampered with a shoulder in-jury and he knew he was heading back to junior hockey for more seasoning. At the same time, Lyle's desire to make the NHL was turned up a notch. "It was just amazing. It really put everything together for me," he said. "Once you get there, you never want to leave." Still, he recognized he was headed back to junior no matter what. "I was only 18. There was no way I was going to crack that lineup. I couldn't believe how fat it was, how tough the guys were." Selmar's NHL career would be only 18 games long over a number of seasons. He said injuries, in particular a knee, did it. He had three operations on the knee by the age of 20 and has not even been able to jog since. "I really don't have any regrets, but maybe I should have taken better care of myself as a junior," he said. At the same time, he did complete his career with four seasons in Europe, two in Austria, and two in England, where the pressure was off and the fun back in the game.

Lee looked at hockey in a different light, seeing the opportunity for the game to offer him an education. While Medicine Hat in the WHL was interested, he chose the Saskatchewan Junior Hockey League after midget. "I was more leading toward a U.S. scholarship," he said, something not granted to players who have played major junior. He headed to Nipawin and then Yorkton. While in Yorkton, Lee and the Terriers would meet in one of the more notable playoff series in the league's long history. The Terriers lost a six-game set to Notre Dame in the spring of 1988. The Hounds, led by future NHL standout Curtis Joseph, were on their way to winning the Centennial Cup as national champions.

After the Terriers, instead of a U.S. scholarship, Lee headed to SAIT in Calgary, transferring to Concordia, before the lure of professional hockey finally captured him. A call came from Steve Carlson, one of the famed Hanson Brothers in the hockey cult-favourite film *Slapshot*. Carlson was coaching the Jamestown Chiefs, also famed from the same movie. The Chiefs were in the East Coast Hockey League and Lee said the action wasn't so far removed from that of the movie. "My first shift my defence partner gets stuck. Of course I had to go help him and there's a line brawl. I spent the whole season with a black eye on one side of my face or the other. I think on every road trip we watched the movie, too. It was great."

When his junior career was complete in Regina, Lyle headed to Montreal, making a pit stop in the minors his first season. It was with the Peoria Rivermen of the International Hockey League that he scored his first professional goal, on his first shift, taking his first shot. It came against Tim Cheveldae, whom he had faced in the WHL. The time in the minors was good, said Lyle, especially with veterans around to learn from. "You watched and learned, and fed off everything and things started rolling and clicking."

Once Lyle made the jump to the NHL, he was there to stay, and it would be a long stay, too. His first seven seasons would be as a Canadien, including the Stanley Cup win of the 1992–93 season. "It was unbelievable. You work so hard to get there," he said of the Cup win. At the time he was young and felt he'd get another one someday. "I haven't been back to the dance since." In the case of the Canadiens that season, while anchored by star goaltender Patrick Roy, the team was short on superstars, but deep in work ethic. As a result, they won 10 overtime games in the playoffs. In fact, in the finals, they dropped the series opener to Los Angeles, then won the next three in overtime, before winning the Cup in five games. "We weren't a great team, just a character bunch of guys who worked hard every night, and everything fell into place," said Lyle. That made the win a little sweeter in his mind. "You realize what you can do with a lot of character guys, what can happen if you outwork the other team."

After the Canadiens, Lyle has become something of a realtor's dream in the NHL, spending time in New Jersey, Phoenix, Columbus, Chicago, Dallas, and, as of the 2003–04 season,

Florida. He said he has tried to take the myriad of trades with a positive mindset, noting he has often moved at the trade deadline to a team looking for another piece of the puzzle to get to the Stanley Cup. "I look at it in a positive way: They have wanted me."

With Florida, Lyle reached a career milestone, becoming the 197th player to play in 1,000 regular-season NHL games. It has taken 15 seasons, but it's a highlight he said he has wanted to achieve for some time. "It's something I really wanted to get to," he said.

Over the years, Lyle has been able to move away from the fights, a trend started in New Jersey, where he was told to stay on the ice more and out of the penalty box. He has become a recognized stay-at-home defenceman, highlighted by being named in 1996 to Canada's World Cup team, the first year of the format bringing the best professional players together to represent their home countries. Ahead, Lyle only sees more hockey at present, logging 20 minutes a game for the Panthers and feeling his best in years. "It's been great. I don't have to fight every three games anymore," he said, adding that there are no regrets about playing tough. "You do what you have to do to survive."

Since he retired in 1994, Selmar has never played the game, although he does skate with his two youngest sons and his daughter. His eldest son, Scott Odelein, has grown into a junior career playing with the La Ronge Icewolves of the Saskatchewan Junior Hockey League. And Selmar has spent time coaching, following Scott all the way to AA Bantam on the bench. It's almost full circle for Selmar, a point his father made some years ago. "Dad asked me if I was crazy when the kids started wearing skates," he joked.

For Lee, survival in the game meant a trip across the Atlantic to play for the Bracknell Bees in the British elite league for the 1991–92 season, after two-and-a-half seasons in the minors of hockey in North America. Twelve games into his British season, his career would come to an ugly end. "I was cross-checked across the back of the head. I was out cold. The guy jumped on me and started banging my head onto the ice. He broke my cheek bone, my eye socket, my nose," he said, adding that the incident made headlines. "When I woke up in the hospital, there was a policeman standing there." The offending player, Roger Hunt, was to be charged with causing gross bodily harm, although he had already left Britain, where he was banned from hockey for life. Lee said in about 2000, he did get a call asking if he minded if the ban was lifted and he said he didn't. At the time, though, Lee faced plastic surgery and the realization his playing days were pretty well over.

However, an interesting opportunity rose for Lee, who was handed the job as player coach and manager of a Division III team in Bristol. Along with the team, he was responsible for organizing three minor teams, down to an under-10 squad and a women's team in the British city. "It was a real challenge, but I enjoyed it," he said. However, when an opportunity came up to coach the next season for his old junior team in Yorkton, he took it. Lee eventually took the Terriers to a league final in 1996 against Melfort, losing with a battered lineup that included captain Neil Schell out after losing a kidney in an on-ice injury. "We just ran out of gas against Melfort. I still believe we were the better team ... We had a really good group of players, experienced and talented." The Terriers would earn a pass into the Royal Bank Cup in Melfort even after losing the SJHL finals, but came up short there as well.

After five seasons with Yorkton, Lee moved onto Winston-Salem in the United Hockey League and more bad luck. The team was stumbling when he took over, but turned around to make the playoffs, leading their first series when the money ran out. It was so bad that there was no money to make a road trip had the series continued. "We didn't play that hard the last game because we couldn't afford the bus to go back to play another game," he said. "It's tough when you get the players to go to battle for you and then you run out of money." It was enough to put Lee on the path to non-hockey employment. "From there, I decided that was enough. I was tired of riding the bus ... I miss the competitiveness of the coaching, but I don't miss the politics."

Mr. Red Wing

When it comes to coaching hockey in Saskatchewan, no one is better known or more respected than Dwight McMillan. His reputation is well-earned, much of it coming from years behind the bench of the Saskatchewan Junior Hockey League Weyburn Red Wings.

McMillan began coaching in 1966 with the Junior B team in Weyburn, and he spent four seasons with the city's midget program, which included an opportunity to coach a young Dave "Tiger" Williams. The two teams proved a training ground for what lay ahead. In the fall of 1972, McMillan stepped behind the Wings' SJHL bench and, with the exception of a couple of seasons away from the team, he has remained there since.

What has kept him on the bench for more than a quarter of a century is something of a mystery, even to the man himself. "I've never really sat down and thought about what it is that keeps me coaching," he said when asked. "I guess it's the challenge of winning and of developing young men." McMillan likened coaching to "going to war," where at the end of each on-ice battle must come a time of reflection. "When you win one you sit down and figure out how to win the next one. If you lose, you look at what you did wrong so you can fix it to win the next one."

In February 2004, McMillan entered the realms of coaching immortality. A 5–3 win over the Melville Millionaires on home ice was McMillan's 900th career win. That put him third on the all-time list of junior coaching wins behind Bert Templeton, who ended his career with 907 wins, and Brian Kilrea of the Ottawa 67s. Kilrea won his 1,000th game in March 2003.

McMillan was in his 25th full season with the Wings when the milestone was achieved. He has won 40 or more games in a season on nine occasions. The Wings with McMillan on the bench have captured six SJHL championships (now called the MemberCARE Cup). McMillan took the milestone win with his characteristic humble attitude. He likened it to simply going to work for 900 days, suggesting that longevity alone will earn one such marks. "It's something I never thought about," he said. The win could have come and gone without his notice, if not for the media and others. "The 900 wins don't help me win the next game."

Among the hundreds of wins, one probably stands at the forefront, the 1984 Wings victory over the Orillia Travelways in the Centennial Cup (now the Royal Bank Cup) final, symbolic of a Canadian championship. "You don't win a national championship everyday," said McMillan, an understatement considering Saskatchewan has won only two titles since the Wings turned the trick—Notre Dame in 1988 and Humboldt in 2003. McMillan said timing has a lot to do with winning. "The year before, I thought we actually had a better club," he said, noting that injuries as the regular season ended and the playoffs began grounded the Wings' chances. The Wings would make a second finals appearance in 1998, losing to the South Surrey Eagles. It's one game

McMillan said he would wish back as he looks over his career. "Their goaltender was MVP of the tournament and he certainly stood on his head that game. We had numerous great scoring chances and he stole it from us."

In 2005, the Royal Bank Cup will be played in Weyburn, meaning the Wings get an automatic spot in the tournament. While admitting he'd love a Wing win, he sees more in hosting the event, too. "I want it to be a first-class Royal Bank Cup," he said, suggesting that the event will be a showcase for the community and the league. Still, you know his heart beats a bit faster thinking of a national win on home ice. "It's a one-time shot," he said. Admittedly, McMillan said winning the title is hard coming from the SJHL, the junior league he believes is the best in the country, even if it is a biased point of view. "It's tough coming out of this league. You have very difficult playoff games here. You can be pretty banged up by the time you get there," he said. "The opportunity to win your way to the Royal Bank Cup is a tough road in Canada. It's a long, hard drag. The thing is usually what we've been faced with and that is you're not fresh for the tournament," he said. "And you're faced with lots of different rules ... like you can't have your names on your jerseys. Those things seem to keep you busy and sort of disrupt what players are used to."

Ultimately, come a playoff game or any other contest, players need to want to win. "Work ethic is the number one thing we've got to have. That's got to be with us every night," said McMillan in an interview prior to the start of the 2003 SJHL playoffs. McMillan, who has only missed the playoffs two or three times as coach, said his experience can at times play a role, but it really has to come from the players by playoff time. "It really has to come from within," he said in 2003. "If they're in the right mode and it's working, I believe you let them go at it." Coaching becomes more critical when a team is not on its game. "You try to draw on your experience and try things. It doesn't always work, but you hope that you punch the right buttons."

While McMillan has risen to prominence as coach of the Red Wings, his association with the team goes back to its very origins. The Wings first took flight in 1961, sponsored by the National Hockey League's Detroit Red Wings, and McMillan was there as a player in the team's first year. "I didn't know a thing about the league or Weyburn when I left Lashburn," he said, having grown up in the small Saskatchewan community in an era before hockey players were travelling across the province every weekend, even as kids, to play. "I just got on the bus and went."

For McMillan, hockey really started at a small rural school called Bear Island. "The fathers there built a rink every year," he said. From there, Mr. Prout took over, a teacher who believed athletics were a large part of education. "In the morning we cleared the rink and at noon we played for an hour-and-a-half." On Sundays, too, the outdoor rink became a centrepiece for community activities. "It was the big sports event for the community. I remember people were still coming with horses and cutters back then." When McMillan matured to the point of playing with the Wings, he came under the tutelage of Stan Dunn. "I learned a million good things from him. He was a great coach and a great man."

McMillan learned enough as a junior that he progressed to the East Coast Hockey League, playing three seasons in the Long Island area, before a veteran headed back down the ladder from the New York Rangers gave the young players on the team some advice. "He told us young guys unless we were sure we were going to make it to the NHL and some good money, we best get our asses out of there and go do something worthwhile," said McMillan. Upon inward reflection, McMillan knew he wasn't going to be the next Gordie Howe, or even Bob Nevin, so he headed home to Weyburn, where he settled into a 37-year job and turned to coaching.

Along the road, McMillan has coached hundreds of players, but the ones who stick in the mind the most are those who developed more than may have been expected over their junior careers. The first name to come out is Barry Melrose from Kelvington, Saskatchewan. Not the most talented player, Melrose would find a way to take his career to both the former World Hockey Association and the NHL, playing 478 games between the two leagues. After his playing days, he started coaching in the Western Hockey League, again advancing to be a head coach in the NHL. McMillan said seeing a player make the most of the opportunities presented through hard work is always gratifying. "He (Melrose) came a long way from when he got here."

It's a case where, as a coach, McMillan said he wants to see a kid succeed when he joins the Wings. "Anybody can cut a kid or fire a guy from work. It takes something more to get the effort and give him the knowledge to make something for himself." When a player leaves the Wings, McMillan said he wants the player to be ready for what comes next, be it college hockey, the pros, senior hockey back home, or, most important, life in general. "When a kids leaves you want him to get to the best level he can."

For McMillan, the first step in helping players achieve is finding a certain type of individual who fits "the Red Wing mould." "Our belief is, character is number one and talent is number two," he said, adding with some sadness that character players are becoming harder to find. "It certainly is. It's just the way society is these days. It's the way commitment and discipline is changing these days." Those same societal changes mean that what worked as a coach in 1972 doesn't work today. "You constantly have to make changes," said McMillan. The key is balancing what is acceptable to players, parents, and fans with what is successful on the ice.

For McMillan, coaching is a way of life. He said he's not into curling or golf, but loves the game of hockey. He has no idea how long he may coach for. "I've been saying for a few years I'll quit when I don't get excited about the game anymore, when I don't want to go to the rink anymore, when I don't get mad when we don't play hard." Coaching isn't easy, but it has become a passion. "You're going to win some, and you're (going to) lose some. I tell young guys starting in as coaches, 'There will be lots of lows, as well as ups. If you're not prepared to handle that, you shouldn't be in the business.'"

Chevy Shines in Motor City

Tim Cheveldae's hockey journey has come full circle. Cheveldae rose to prominence with the Saskatoon Blades of the Western Hockey League, where from 1985 to 1988 he recorded 85 wins as the team's top goaltender. The 85 wins set a record among Blade goaltenders that remains intact to this day.

Nearly 20 years since he first donned a Blades uniform, Cheveldae admitted specific memories have faded. "I find the whole time as a bit of a blur," he said, adding that he does know the time with Saskatoon was a special one. "The team I'm most proud of playing with was the Saskatoon Blades." The team might not have had the list of stars some teams in the league had at the time, said Cheveldae, but it was still successful. "We just did it as a team. I think we got everything we could as a team," he said.

It was Saskatoon Blade coach Murcel Comeau who put the finishing touches on Cheveldae. "In my second year of junior hockey (1986–'87), when I didn't have a lot of confidence in myself, he showed confidence in me and just kept putting me back in there, playing me until he got me back on track. I really appreciate what he did for me, because when you're in junior hockey, you're sort of at a crossroads and you can go either one way or the other," he said.

The work ethic of the Blades was not lost on Cheveldae, who recited an old adage of the game, "Work beats talent, unless talent works." On a personal level, that translated into an understanding that he would need to work, too. "I believe you have a better understanding of what it takes to be successful after playing with a team like the Blades were," he said. Of course, many of the best lessons about hockey were learned while he was a kid back in his hometown of Melville.

Cheveldae said it was never really in his mind to guard the cage, but when he was put into net for a game, his fate was set. "I got a shutout my very first game," he said. He always appreciated the early games of minor hockey as he progressed in his career. "It was huge. You've got to have a foundation," said Cheveldae. "You've got to have a start on your career."

Cheveldae credited his playing time in Melville's minor hockey system as a key building block in making him an NHLer. "They gave me the opportunity to play. They gave me ice time. If you're going to improve you have to have the good quality of hockey to play against," he said. "One of the biggest reasons—but you didn't think about it at the time—was we didn't have very good hockey teams, so I faced a lot of shots. It was probably a blessing in disguise that I had a lot of chances to practise."

Melville Minor Sports also gets a big thank-you from Cheveldae, because they supplied youngsters with goaltending equipment. "If my family had to buy the equipment, I probably wouldn't have been a goaltender," he said. At the same time, just playing hockey in Saskatchewan, where minus 40-degree weather makes for cold road trips and cold rinks, helped Cheveldae develop as a player. "I think it helps mould a player when you may have to endure a few more hardships," he said. "When you have to go when it's 40 below ... it helps build character." Such hardships help when you hit a big city such as Detroit and it takes 35 minutes to get from your home to the rink. "In 35 minutes you could drive from Melville to Yorkton. So it's a whole different experience," said Cheveldae. "So you try to remember what it was like to be a kid, remember what you learned."

Cheveldae is now back with the Blades as the team's goaltender coach. "I found it very exciting to come back," he said. Cheveldae realized at an early age that coaching was something he wanted to do when his playing career was over. "I wanted to be a coach when I was 24 or 25. I've always enjoyed the Xs and Os of hockey," he said. "I saw it as an opportunity to give something back, way before I was done playing." At the same time, no one coach stands out as a key influence he now draws on as he works with young netminders. "From every coach you have, there are things you pick up," said Cheveldae, adding that what he does try to do is look at what commonalities successful coaches have. "They pay attention to the little things, the little details," he said. Of course, some warrant closer scrutiny, including Dave Lewis, a long-time assistant and then head coach in Detroit. "He's a great person. He's been around the game so long (1,000 career games). He has a lot of insights," said Cheveldae. "I really respect him, his opinions, his views."

Coaching has taken Cheveldae into a different aspect of the game he loves. "After a playing career you certainly have a different outlook on what it takes to be a coach," he said. The difference comes in how a player views the game and how a coach views the same situation. "Players see a lot of things in black and white," said Cheveldae. "As a coach you have to see a lot of things in shades of grey." Cheveldae said he is still learning about the position he played for years, even now as he coaches others in the skills of the position. "I've probably learned more about goaltending after becoming a coach, at least on the technical side, than I did as a player," he said. As a coach, too, Cheveldae said it's a case of finding how to motivate the young netminders he works with. "Every goaltender is different," he said. "You're trying to find the right buttons to push to help the goaltenders focus." So what buttons did coaches push to get Cheveldae to roll up all the wins he had when he was a Blade? "I was pretty self-motivated. I was pretty hard on myself," he said. Cheveldae said as a goaltender he realized early on that his position was the one on the team where, as an individual, he could win or lose a game on his own performance. "I didn't want to be the reason we lost on any given night," said Cheveldae.

Between his times with the Blades as player and coach, Cheveldae carved out a solid, but at the same time somewhat disappointing, National Hockey League career. That Cheveldae would spend only a year and a half in the minors—Adirondack of the American Hockey League—was also unexpected. "I know a lot of good goalies in the minor systems and they never had the chance because other (NHL) teams have good one-two goalies," he said. "I was fortunate. You need that little luck and you need the break. I think the only way goalies can get better is by getting the chance to play and Bryan Murray (Red Wing coach and GM) had given me that opportunity the last two years."

Cheveldae was drafted in the fourth round, 64th overall, by the Detroit Red Wings in the 1986 draft. By the 1990–91 season, Cheveldae was the go-to man in Detroit, ruling the roost and the media for the next three seasons. In 1991–92, his stock was so high in Detroit that he played 4,236 minutes in over 72 games played, recording 38 wins with a goals-against average of 3.20. In only his second full NHL season, Cheveldae played in the 1991–92 all-star game, an experience he won't soon forget. "It was a big thrill," he said in 1992. "The thing I'm going to remember is walking in the dressing room and seeing guys like Brett Hull, Wayne Gretzky, Larry Robinson, and Doug Wilson, guys who are going to be in the Hall of Fame."

Cheveldae, who helped backstop the Wings to 98 points, third overall in the league in 1991–92, admitted then that playing in the NHL was a dream come true. "I think anytime you lace on the skates as a little kid you dream of playing in the NHL. It certainly was my dream," he said in a 1992 interview. "I think we still have a few years ahead, but you don't want to waste those years. You always want to go as far as you can when you're playing." Sometimes you don't go as far as you might expect. Two seasons later he was a Winnipeg Jet, and by 1998, he was out of hockey after a season with the International Hockey League Las Vegas Thunder. Cheveldae admitted his career ended before it should have, especially in Detroit, where for a short time the man called "Chevy" was a hot commodity. "When I look back on my time in Detroit, there were negatives, but I try to look more at the positive situations," he said. Certainly there were positives to hold on to. "The opportunity to play in the all-star game was one of the highlights of my NHL career," he said.

Cheveldae's first win is committed to memory as well. It came in St. Louis on a night when the Wings trailed 3–1 going into the third period, but ended up winning 4–3. "I think you remember certain games," he said, adding that there was a playoff game in Minnesota that stands out. The Wings trailed the series four games to three. "We ended up winning the game 1–0 in overtime," said Cheveldae. "That's very special for a goaltender."

Some opponents remain fresh in the memory, too. Not surprisingly, Mario Lemieux topped the list when asked who was the toughest shooter he faced. Thankfully, he added, the Wings and Pittsburgh Penguins didn't face off that often during his career. By contrast, Detroit did play St. Louis eight or 10 times a season, said Cheveldae, which meant facing Brett Hull and his linemate Adam Oates. "That was the time Hull was scoring 70," said Cheveldae, who added it was never fun facing his howitzer of a shot.

But it was all over too soon for Cheveldae, who said he laments his career did not last longer. "Unfortunately, I do (have regrets)," he said, "Certainly, I'm proud that I played in the NHL, but obviously there are things I would have done differently during my career." The first change he'd make would be to ignore what was being written and said on television about his play. "The big thing for me, I got caught up in the media," he said. In retrospect, Cheveldae said he forgot to just worry about what he was doing on the ice, as an NHL goaltender. "You have to learn to just focus on the things you have control over," he said. "I didn't have much control over what media said."

Now that his professional career is over, Cheveldae rarely straps on the pads these days. There is no recreational hockey on his weekly winter schedule, although a good cause will lure him to unpack the gear. "I don't play a lot anymore," he said. "Just an occasional charity game." He wishes now he had stayed playing the game longer. "Playing hockey is the greatest life you can have," he said. "But sometimes you don't stop and smell the roses." Cheveldae hung up the skates at 30, young in comparison to many in the game today. He said that if he were to do it over, he would likely have played a few more seasons, in spite of good reasons to retire. "I wasn't enjoying the game anymore. I wasn't happy about the level I was playing at," he said. "I had moved four times in four years and it was pretty hard on my family. They made a lot of sacrifices, so I thought it was time to put some roots down and gets things settled." So what's next for Cheveldae? It's a question even he struggles with. He enjoys coaching, but has no interest in yet another move with his family, so he knows that may limit opportunities to advance to head coaching status. "I would like to try my hand as a head coach," he said. At the same time, coaching is a connection to a game he loves and misses. "One thing you miss is not being in the dressing room, just being with the guys," said Cheveldae. "You really miss that when you're not playing. Coaching helps you get some of that back."

Sage of the SJHL

For more than a quarter of a century, Wayne Kartusch and the Saskatchewan Junior Hockey League (SJHL) were synonymous. It was in 1971 that Kartusch first took over the role of SJHL president on the suggestion of long-time hockey associate Stan Dunn, who was at the time coaching in Swift Current. Kartusch himself was on the bench of the Regina Pat Canadians, the SJHL affiliate farm team of the Western Hockey League Pats. It was a position he had held for six years. "He (Dunn) said, 'Why don't you take a run at being our league president?'" recalled Kartusch, who added he liked the idea enough to give the position a one-year commitment.

"I went on a year-to-year basis for the next 20 years," said Kartusch, each of those years holding the position of president on a part-time basis. Then for six years, before retiring following the 2002-03 season, he would hold the position full-time. "It was just getting to be too much work on a part-time basis. There wasn't time for proper preparation, and the legwork some things required," he said. "It (going full-time) certainly opened the door and made it so more attention could be paid to details."

While Kartusch admitted "never in a million years" did he expect to hold the position of president for 26 years, his varied background made him a rather obvious choice to assume the role in the first place. A Regina product, Kartusch played in the early edition of the league he would one day oversee. "I played junior hockey for the Pats when that team was part of the Saskatchewan junior league," he said. Kartusch showed enough skill as a player that he was awarded a hockey scholarship at the University of Michigan, heading south in 1960 at a time when the university was part of the only elite league in U.S. college hockey, with teams such as Michigan State, North Dakota University, Minnesota, and Colorado College. He would spend four years at the school, through a time when the team had some half-dozen Regina players, including Red Berenson. "The hockey was like a progression from junior. It was mostly players who had completed their junior careers," he said, adding that the situation made college hockey a slightly older league than it is today.

As for playing with Berenson, who would go on to a notable National Hockey League career, Kartusch said he recalled his teammate's final game in a national final played in upstate New York. "Sam Pollock and Claude Ruel were right there after the game to pick him (Berenson) up and take him up to the Montreal Canadiens," he said. Following his time at Michigan, Kartusch, who took education, headed to the pro ranks, playing in the International Hockey League with Windsor in the team's only year in the IHL. "The previous year they had won the Allan Cup, and they and Chatham, decided to turn pro," said Kartusch. The season was a rough one to the extent he termed it "right out of *Slapshot*," the cult movie hockey classic. The next year they both went back to senior hockey. It was enough to send Kartusch to the University of Pittsburgh in search of his master's degree.

However, once back in Regina, Kartusch was back on the ice, too. "I played senior hockey the first couple of years back," he said. While toiling with the Senior Regina Caps, Kartusch also moved behind the bench for the first time with the Regina Pat Bs, a team in the Seven Plains League that included both Junior B and intermediate-level teams.

The next step for Kartusch was away from playing, instead keeping his skates sharpened for his new ice endeavour as a referee. Kartusch said a hockey associate said he was an ideal candidate to don the stripes. "He said I'd be a good referee because I probably knew all the rules 'because you've broken them all.'" He admitted he was probably most noted as a rough and ready player. Having been a player who liked to at least push the rules made Kartusch what he said was sort of a player's ref, allowing teams to play the game without blowing the whistle too often. "That was what I was told was my characteristic as a ref. I had a feel for what the players wanted and I let them play," he said. "I liked doing games with good tough hockey and very few penalties. Sometimes it got you in trouble, but most of the time it worked."

Kartusch would wear the ref's uniform for some six seasons in what would become the Western Hockey League. He moved back behind the bench in 1971 as coach of the Regina Pat Blues in the SJHL for the six years leading up to assuming the president's mantle. Kartusch struggles with the question of his number one memory of being the league president for 26 years. "I've been asked that so often and I can't pick out any one thing. Every year had its satisfaction and disappointments." What Kartusch does remember fondly are the people. "There are so many good people with the teams. Sometimes they're rather colourful people, but they're still good people."

However, each person of course comes to the SJHL board table with the interests of their own teams fresh in their minds. Kartusch said that was at times a challenge in itself, where he found he had to be a consensus builder. "You had to get them to think out of their own box, and think about the big picture," he said. He was sure that was the case in any league. Kartusch is also proud of the way the SJHL has grown as a league. "The growth of the league, and the stability of it, is rewarding."

But even with the general strength of the league, Kartusch has seen several teams come and go, several of those moves leaving their impression in his memories. In most sport leagues, teams fold for a variety of reasons, and Kartusch saw that occur several times with the SJHL, including the league finally leaving the province's two major cities of Regina and Saskatoon. That process really started when the WHL teams in those cities dropped their farm teams, the Regina Blues and Saskatoon Jays. Other teams would try their way in the major centres, but could never compete for fans with the Western League. Three communities also left the league to join the Western loop, with Prince Albert, Moose Jaw, and Swift Current taking the step. These moves allowed the SJHL to become what Kartusch said is the strength of leagues of its kind. "It became what Junior A hockey is right across the country—small, community-based hockey."

Of course, being community-based provides challenges to the team and to the league. "In our particular case, all the teams are operated by volunteers," said Kartusch, explaining that the volunteers essentially have to work all day and then show up at the rink at night to keep their team operating. "That's a big challenge for the communities and for the league, too," he said, noting that teams can see volunteers tire and move on rather quickly. "But there always seemed somebody would be there to pick up the ball for another two or three years."

When it came to good organizations, Kartusch said the SJHL certainly lost one when the Prince Albert Raiders moved to the Western loop. Under the guidance of coaches such as Terry Simpson and Rick Wilson, the team excelled, dominating the SJ for several years before moving on. It was a case of the community and the team being almost inseparable. "The players were part of the community. And it meant something to be on the executive of the Raiders and wear that green jacket around the city," said Kartusch.

While some teams grew to another league, others couldn't keep things afloat and eventually folded. One of the communities that failed was located in Minot, North Dakota, as part of the SJHL's move into the United States. "We knew the odds were going to be stiff," said Kartusch. "And things just got off to the worst possible start of any franchise." Minot was playing in their first season in Estevan when a young player, an American high school student, was taken into the boards and his neck broken. "I don't think the team ever overcame that," said Kartusch. The American experiment was a disappointment, said Kartusch, adding that he believed that had Minot been successful, communities such as Williston and Bismark would have followed. "Both of those centres had expressed interest." Kartusch said it was also disappointing to see the Lebret Eagles, a team run by First Nations people, fold. "What happened there should never have happened. It was such a benefit to have a team like that in the league. It was a great organization for the native community to look up to. It's too bad it had to fold."

One thing Kartusch does expect, as he looks ahead to what his successor Laury Ryan may face as president, is more changes in which teams remain in the league. "It's getting tougher and tougher in communities of four- or five-thousand people to support a team," he said, adding that the smaller communities don't have the corporate support of larger centres and find it more difficult to attract players. When it comes to players, Kartusch said finding talent is increasingly a challenge across hockey, and at the junior level there may simply be too many teams vying for an ever-shallower talent pool. "There are fewer kids playing hockey. I think the talent pool is becoming more limited," he said. "You see that all the way up to the NHL."

Costs are also a concern, with teams needing minimum budgets of $300,000 a year now. The cost is significantly higher in the WHL, and Kartusch said it wouldn't surprise him if, in the next half-decade, some of the teams that moved up to the Western League return to the SJHL fold as a more affordable brand of quality hockey. For any league, success, especially on the national stage, is gratifying. In the case of the SJHL, it has had teams in the Royal Bank Cup (formerly Centennial Cup) Tournament on numerous occasions, although they didn't win the crown as often as Kartusch may have desired. "We didn't always win it, but we certainly had our share of opportunities." Each visit to the national stage was a credit to the team and the league, suggested Kartusch. "It's a tribute to the team and also a tribute to the league. You can't get there by yourself. You have to have good competition to prepare for the next level."

One team that sticks in Kartusch's mind is the Notre Dame Hounds, who won the title in 1988 in the team's first year in the SJHL. "That was totally unbelievable," said Kartusch. He said he recalls attending the Canadian Hockey Association annual meeting in the spring of 1987 and reporting that Notre Dame would be in the SJHL that fall. Someone from Ontario remarked, "Yeah, and they'll probably win the national championship, too." It proved a bang-on prediction. "That was just a phenomenal team," said Kartusch, relating how exciting it was to see the Hounds come back from a 3–1 deficit to Calgary to take that series in seven games on Calgary ice to advance. In the deciding game, Curtis Joseph, who went on to the NHL, had to stop a penalty shot late in the third period to ensure the win. It was a feat Kartusch said he repeated again in Halifax in the finals tournament.

In Kartusch's mind, Joseph was the best goaltender he saw during his tenure as SJHL president. "Undoubtedly. He was a character goaltender and just a super kid, on and off the ice." When it comes to unforgettable, Kartusch also speaks highly of Weyburn Red Wing coach Dwight McMillan, who recorded his 900th junior win the season after Kartusch's retirement. "It was great to see. It shows the dedication he has to this game and to junior hockey. To reach 900 wins at any level is remarkable. His dedication and perseverance is amazing," said Kartusch.

With much to be proud of, from league stability to championship teams, Kartusch said he certainly misses being involved. "No question I miss it," he said. In his first season away, he headed to Mexico for five weeks just to stay well away from the rink. At the same time, Kartusch said he believes he left at the appropriate time. "I think the league was left in pretty good shape," he said modestly.

The Buckaroo From Bangor

The now-defunct Western Hockey League boasted a high calibre of players for years, with teams throughout Western Canada and the United States. One of the true standouts of the league was a slightly built forward, born in Bangor, Saskatchewan, who cut his hockey teeth in Saskatoon as a boy. Art Jones weighed only 150 pounds as a 20-year-old when he left Saskatoon for a tryout in Spokane. By 1957, he was a rookie in the old WHL, scoring 29 goals and 66 points in New Westminster, not bad numbers, but just a hint of what was to come. Before his career ended, with the demise of the league itself in 1974, Jones would lead the WHL in scoring on six occasions. He would also earn the George Leader Trophy as the league's Most Valuable Player for the 1967–68 and the 1970–71 seasons.

When asked about his 18-season career in the WHL, Jones was modest, with an added twist of humour. "I did all right. I had a lot of fun," he said. "But I didn't make a lot of money." While the career he carved out was a good one, Jones credits outdoor rinks and good competition in Saskatoon for his success. "My brothers

(Gordon and Newton) taught me how to play," recalled Jones, adding that his start in the game came in goal. It was a position he wasn't destined to play for long. "I guess I was pretty smart," he said with a laugh. "I moved right away. I got out of goal when I was five or six years old."

While still a teenager, Jones joined a team he said made him the player he was. "We formed a barnstorming team that went around to all the little towns and played their senior teams," he said. The competition in towns such as Davidson and Allan was such that Jones's skills were well honed. "I think a lot of it was playing against older guys in those little towns," said Jones. "There were a lot of good players out there. That's when I learned all my skills, playing against those guys." The barnstorming team would last only one season, after which he would join the Saskatoon Wesleys, a junior team in the city. That, too, would be a one-season stop, thanks to the connections of Wesleys coach Doug Bentley. "His brother Scoop Bentley played in Spokane. He came out to watch us back then and he talked to Rob McBride in Spokane about me," said Jones. An offer was made for a tryout and Jones was on the bus headed south, a decision he said took no time at all. "Not at all. It was getting cold out," he said with a chuckle. "It was no decision at all. I loved playing hockey." Even Jones's parents weren't against the move, although it was hundreds of miles away. "I was 20 by then. They didn't have too much say in the decision," he said, adding that they might have been happy to see him go since he was the youngest and last of the family to leave home.

When Jones arrived in Spokane for the tryout with the Flyers, he found a senior league waiting for him, and that meant a big change in hockey. "It was a lot faster. There were a lot bigger players, and a lot meaner," he said, adding, "I was 150 pounds soaking wet." Was speed then the key for Jones? He suggested not. "Not speed, but finesse, I guess you'd call it," he said. That first-season finesse resulted in some 44 goals and about 40 assists, "not bad for a 20-year-old," said Jones. It was an understatement given that he was lining up against some players nearly twice his age. In fact, Jones was so young, he was kind of alone on the team. "I didn't have too many friends on the team. I couldn't even get into any taverns to drink with them," he said. "I was pretty well on my own."

Fortunately, Jones ended up with an almost mother, or perhaps grandmother, as his landlady that first season. "(She) was a little old lady who was a hockey fan. She was about 80 years old," he said, adding that the rent was a whopping $33.10 per month. "All I had to do was stoke the stove." It wasn't a bad arrangement for a young player, and the rent was definitely right, considering he was making $400 a week to play.

While with Spokane, Jones was part of the first American team to play for the fabled Allan Cup, symbol of supremacy in senior hockey in Canada. The team had to play in Ontario, defeating Thunder Bay on their way to Toronto. When they arrived in Toronto, they found they had to wait for the Whitby Dunlops to finish their run to the Cup final, a situation that dragged on for weeks. "We had to wait a whole month for them," said Jones. "All we did was sit around the hotel and look stupid." Looking back, Jones said the delay may have been to make sure an American team didn't win the Allan Cup. With no ice to even practise on, the ploy worked. Jones related how Spokane's goaltender, John Sofiak, also a Saskatoon native, weighed 190 pounds during the season, but ballooned to 250 by the start of the series with Whitby at Maple Leaf Gardens. "They took us four straight," said Jones, adding that it was too bad they were embarrassed by the situation. "They probably would have beat us anyway. The Dunlops won the World Championships the next year (1958)."

The next season Jones was on the move to New Westminster, a team that would transfer in two seasons to become the Portland

Buckaroos, his long-time WHL home. The move to the B.C. team came at the request of the Toronto Maple Leafs, the National Hockey League team that had signed him to what was called a C card, which didn't mean a whole lot for most players in those days. "They sent me a hundred dollars every year," said Jones. When Jones and a core group of players finally arrived in Portland in the fall of 1960, they started play in a brand-new arena, replacing one that had been condemned about a decade earlier. "For almost 10 years they didn't have a rink," said Jones, adding that the new rink was huge. "It was the biggest rink in the WHL for eight or nine years. The fan support was there, too. The first game there were about 3,500 people. It really took off. There were soon 10,500," he said. "In the playoffs police were at the doors trying to stop people from sneaking in."

For the next 14 seasons, Jones was a happy Buckaroo. "We had a tremendous league. The NHL teams used to come out here to play against a lot of the teams in the league," he said. One year Jones recalled Toronto coming to town after winning the Stanley Cup a year earlier. "We beat them 2–1," he said, adding that he remembers wins over the Boston Bruins and Chicago Black Hawks, too. Jones said the games were big for fans, but nothing particularly special for him. "It was just another game. It didn't seem to be that big at all." At the same time, though, Jones said competing against NHL teams may have pushed the Buckaroos to play better just to show they were every bit as good as the NHLers. "I think that was a lot of it. We were always up for the games," he said. By contrast the games held little interest for the visiting teams. "They came here and weren't really up for the games at all. It wasn't really important to them."

So how close was Jones to playing in the NHL himself? Well, he was drafted by Montreal in 1961, but he said it was a draft never meant to give him a shot at making the Canadiens.

"It turned out it was a spite draft," he said, suggesting personalities were at play and he was drafted simply to get at Hal Layco, who was a supporter and had been in an altercation with Maurice Richard. "So Portland bought me back." Not making the NHL was never a regret. "They didn't make much more money than we did," he said. "Seventy-five-hundred dollars was the league minimum, and I was making more than that down here."

While the seasons rolled by, Jones would score 492 goals and add 869 assists for 1,361 points with the Buckaroos. Overall he would have 1,580 points in the WHL, second careerwise to Guyle Fielder's 1,846. He said a pair of Saskatoon-born brothers played a role in many of his points as an early linemate in Portland—first it was Arnie Schmautz and later it was his brother Clifford Schmautz. Of course, all of the scoring was highlighted by the two league MVP awards. "When you win an award like that it's quite an honour," he said simply. Still, the best memory was his first season in Portland, said Jones, "when we won our first championship." He said it was a sweet win considering a Calgary writer had suggested Portland was the worst team ever to come into the WHL. "We sort of shoved that down his throat."

Jones said the Buckaroos had a good group of players from New Westminster, and two additions, lanky Dale Rolfe, on the verge of a long NHL career, and Don Head, the goaltender who solidified things. Head was coming off a silver medal for Canada at the Olympics in Squaw Valley, California.

In his years with Portland, Jones would be on two more championship teams and in the hunt most years. "I think we only missed the playoffs one year and we were in the finals eight or nine times," he said. So there was some sadness when the league folded out from under him. "I was there until the very end. When the last puck was dropped I was on the ice," he said, adding that it was a loss in the league final, too. He said he wanted to stay playing in

Portland. "I had another year in me. I was 39. I was going to play another season and then give it up." Still living in Oregon, Jones said he watches hockey on television, but can't stand going to the Portland rink to watch the junior Winterhawks. In fact, all hockey is missing something today in his way of thinking. "It's more shoot it in and the biggest guy in the corner gets the puck. It's very boring," said Jones. "It's just a big scrimmage along the glass for a minute and a half, and the biggest guy gets it. There's no finesse anymore. You don't see anyone carry the puck four feet. It's not a pretty game to watch anymore ... And I think we had more fun than these guys ever do."